TRAVELING DOWN THE ROAD

WITH

GRACE

Written by
Joann Grandberry

Illustrations by
Mackenzie Grace Colby

Copyright page

Traveling Down the Road with Grace: A Journey of Love, Resilience, and Discovery
Copyright © 2024 by Joan Wilson

All rights reserved. No part of this book may be reproduced, distributed, or transmitted in any form or by any means, including photocopying, recording, or other electronic or mechanical methods, without the prior written permission of the publisher, except in the case of brief quotations embodied in critical reviews and certain other noncommercial uses permitted by copyright law. For permission requests, please contact the publisher at the address below.

Published by **Get Published Successfully LLC**

" Scripture taken from the NEW AMERICAN STANDARD BIBLE, Copyright C 1995 by The Lockman Foundation. Used by permission www.Locjman.org"

ISBN: 979-8-9918992-0-8

This book is a work of nonfiction. Names, characters, places, and events are portrayed as accurately as possible to the best of the author's knowledge. In certain instances, names of individuals and locations may have been changed to protect privacy. Any resemblance to actual persons, living or deceased, is coincidental.

Printed in the United States of America

First Edition

Traveling Down the Road With Grace

Contents

Copyright page 2
Acknowledgments 5
Book Endorsements 6
Dedication 11
Preface 13
1: A Little Light Shines 17
2: Imprints In The Dirt 22
3: Summertime, Good Times 27
4: Adoption In The Family 30
5: Time 35
6: New Orleans 37
7: The Sunshine State 41
8: Grace Was At The Wedding 46
9: Saved By Grace 49
10: Home In Alabama 54
11: Another Family Adoption 58
12: Everyone Forgets Sometimes! 63
13: Renewed And Restored 67
14: Grace's Flower Garden 70
15: Dealing With The Loneliness 73
16: Mammograms – Two In One Day 76
17: The Coldest Day In January 78
18: Purple for Royalty & Alzheimer's 81
19: May I Present, Queen Grace! 83

20: Laughter And Love 86
21: New England In The Fall 90
22: The Official Tour Begins 94
23: The Splendor Of New England.......................... 117
24: The Magnificent Mountains!............................. 120
25: A Memory From The Past................................... 124
26: The End Of Our New England Tour 127
27: The "Springs" 130
28: Music & Dancing On The Mountains 133
29: He Knew!... 138
30: The Theater, The Second Time 142
31: My Cousin, Bobby (March, 2016) 144
32: Friendships And Baskets................................... 148
33: History Of The Blues 152
34: Motor City Music And Memories...................... 158
35: A Day Of Thanksgiving 163
36: To Grandmother's House 168
37: The Black History Tour...................................... 170
38: A Trip To Paradise 173
39: Sitting On The Back Porch 176
40: Great Grace's Last Train Ride........................... 179
41: The Return Trip.. 186
42: The Message Of Love... 189
43: A Gift From A Stranger 192

Traveling Down the Road With Grace

Acknowledgments
LOVE AND APPRECIATION TO:

Reggie, the best son God could have given me.

Ardina, Sydnee, and Emma,
My Core

Mackenzie Grace,
Illustrator Extraordinaire

Ruth Lewis,
Superior Checker

ALL OF MY DAUGHTERS,
Tremendously Loved Young Ladies

Oak Cliff Bible Fellowship, Life on Life,
When you heard my story, my book became alive.
Traphene Hickman Library, Director, and Staff,
You called me "author" before I knew I was one.
My family, friends, and prayer partners,
your names are written on my heart and
God knows each of you!
THANK YOU,

Joann

Book Endorsements

Wow! **Traveling Down the Road with Grace** is a beautifully written book. The stories are captivating and so descriptive you would think you were with Miss Grace and Joann every mile of their journey as they travel from city to city across the country.

Belinda Allen, author
***I'm Not Telling You What to Do,
But Can I make a Suggestion?***

Reading this book is a journey that I will long remember. As I turn the pages, I feel as though I am traveling with Miss Grace and her daughter. Through their eyes, I see all of the incredible views and share their triumphs with them.

Through the pages of this book, I felt the joy of the mother and daughter as they ascended into a world that is not always easy for the elderly. I enjoyed their genuine, heart-rending stories.

Marva Holman, Rukiya Book Club

Traveling Down the Road with Grace is an enlightening book that offers readers a journey through the rich tapestry of African American history, culture, and traditions. The author masterfully narrates the experiences and travels with her charming mother, Miss Grace, by creating a vivid portrayal that transports readers back into a bygone era of American history.

From the first page to the last, Joann's storytelling captivates with its blend of entertainment and education. As you turn each page, you will find yourself walking alongside Miss Grace on their journeys, experiencing first hand warmth and wisdom that she imparts.

Whether you are an avid reader of historical narratives or someone seeking inspiration from stories rooted in cultural richness, **Traveling Down the Road with Grace** promises an unforgettable literary adventure.

Jocelyn Pinkard,
Co-owner of Hidden History DFW

This book could not arrive at a better time. Joann brought to us truckloads of grace to answer the age-old question: "What is the shortest distance between New York and London?" As your fingers traffic through the journey of Grace, you will soon discover that the answer to that question is "Great Company!" During your voyage, allow your heart to contemplate and capture all the scenery personified by Grace.

Grace that even the longest distance in one's life journey would soon shrink in the midst of great company. Miss Grace teaches us that miles and memories are insufficient to fuel the quality of our relationships, but great company does. It has the power to shrink the longest distance of any journey through the sweet presence of Grace, even as she abides with us and leads us into eternity.

**Dr. Edsel Duréus, Senior Pastor,
Thanksgiving Tabernacle Bible Fellowship,
Cedar Hill, Texas**

As an author myself, when I read a book, I want to be transported to the location, hear the sounds, and feel the textures all around me. I want to be able to empathize with the characters and understand what makes them smile and what makes them cry. I want to know what drives them to pray and to praise God if they are people of Faith. I desire an opportunity to follow their eyes to see the colors and enjoy the smallest of details. **Traveling Down the** Road **with Grace** does this and more! Riding along with Grace's trio through God's country was a privilege!! This journal, turned book, allows you to be pulled in by three delightful generations of God's finest as they embark on a journey across the country by rail.

Just as the **Polar Express** was a magical journey for all aboard that train you will be a part of the grace-infused magical experience, and oh what a wonderful ride indeed! Not only will you see the splendor of aspens pointing skyward and hear the thundering voice of the conductor as the train pulls out of the station. You will see that when we pray, God answers.

If I had more thumbs, I would definitely give this one more than two thumbs up! Read this book and enjoy the ride! You won't be disappointed!

Dr. Beverly Caro Duréus, Esq.

Traveling Down the Road with Grace is an entertaining book about living a good life while aging gracefully. This informative and enjoyable book is loaded with interesting history and travel information. The reader will learn a lot, laugh a bit, smile occasionally, and thoroughly enjoy the travels of a daughter and her mother. This book is a delightful choice for an individual reader and an excellent selection for a Book Club read. It can easily be followed with informative and delightful discussions.

I knew and loved Miss Grace and she was such a delightful lady with a great sense of humor and a positive outlook on life!

C. C. Jackson, The Bookie Club

Traveling Down the Road With Grace

Dedication

With love and appreciation, I dedicate my book to:

Miss Grace, my mother,

Miss Lillian, my grandmother,

Aunt Pank, my other mother.

The best of you lives in me today.

. . and the Spirit of the Lord dwells in all of us!

Thank you, Ladies.

Traveling Down the Road With Grace

STRUGGLES

Sometimes the things
that seem to hurt us the most
are the very things
that bring out
The best in us.
They are the struggles
That helps us discover
The faith we thought we had lost,
The courage to
let go of the past and begin again.
Because challenges help us to see
Who we really are,
Where we want to go,
And what our lives can be
If only we have faith and Keep on trying.

Author Unknown

Preface

TRAVELING DOWN THE ROAD WITH GRACE is a collection of *episodes of the journey with my mother, Grace.* God blessed us with *His Grace,* by weaving more than 70 years of our lives together. When I was a young girl, I wanted to discover the whole wide world, and my mother opened the door to my childhood desire when she took me on a train ride. We left the corner of my little world and explored what appeared to be such enormous and magnificent places.

Throughout the years, we continued to travel, and together, we visited more than half of the states in the United States of America, portions of Canada, and the tropical island nation of Jamaica.

When my mother was diagnosed with early-onset Alzheimer's Disease and breast cancer simultaneously, I became her caregiver. While we continued to travel, an astute counselor suggested journaling our trips and I enthusiastically accepted her idea. Today, I am so thankful because that recommendation is the book that you are currently reading.

During our years together, my mother and I traveled countless miles throughout the country. We viewed the majestic mountain ranges from Estes Park in Colorado, and later, we headed west and rode parallel with the Pacific Ocean for numerous miles from southern California to the northern part of the state of Washington. One year we travelled east and stood on the edges of the Atlantic Ocean when we toured several states in New England. Frequently, my mother and I crossed the mighty Mississippi River and headed south to the land of Dixie.

We enjoyed traveling to the big cities and quaint little towns, where we observed countless scenes of the peaceful lifestyles in America. The further we traveled, the more we discovered, and each trip enriched our lives. During the many years of touring our country, we realized we were never too old to wander and discover more about God's magnificent world. As we journeyed through countless towns and cities, we met a variety of people.

WHEN COVID CAME

For decades, Mamma and I traveled across the country, through big cities and tiny towns, on trains and highways that connected us to places and people in ways we never imagined. Each journey reminded us that the world was a little bigger and more wonderful than we had ever thought—and that there was always something new to see. When COVID-19 arrived, all of that came to a sudden, stunning halt.

For the first time in our lives, we couldn't pack our bags or book a ticket; travel was out of the question. With that, we lost more than our trips—we lost part of the rhythm of our lives. They told folks like us that "the aging population" had the highest risk of getting sick and even dying. We did not need to be told twice; we shut our doors, put away our plans, and hunkered down.

With each passing month, we felt the effects more deeply. We missed our Sunday church services, the weekly social gatherings, the visits to the library, and, most of all, our little mother-daughter outings that filled our days with laughter and stories. From grocery shopping to doctor's visits, everything moved online or became a family-assisted errand.

Thanks to the Zoom calls and home delivery services, we managed well enough, but it was a whole different world. Even after restrictions were lifted, we waited a little longer before venturing out. We had learned to let God guide us; therefore, we stayed patient until we felt it was truly safe. When we finally set foot on a train again, the world felt different somehow. We were different. There is something about living through such turbulent times and coming through it with a transformed appreciation for life. Seeing the world once again, we cherished each view out the window, each bend of the tracks, and each "All aboard!" Now when we travel, I see evidence of God's grace. For us, those mountains are now like His footprints, reminders that He walks with us through every valley and over every peak. COVID taught us to savor our time together and remember that each journey, no matter how small, is a blessing from God.

    I thought Mamma was more amenable and accepting of the changes that had occurred in our lives. She was definitely more confident and willing to do "new things." Truthfully, I was, too! Changes had occurred for both of us. Mamma inspired me and I was willing to pursue new methods to help us overcome the obstacles that occurred with all the changes that happened with our new lifestyle. We were comfortable returning to the familiar, traveling. Riding trains across the country was our favorite mode of travel and once again, we became frequent riders on the trains across the country.

    Come, travel back a few decades with us as you join us on a trip that occurred long ago in a little country train station in rural Alabama. Enjoy the journey!

This book was inspired by real-life incidents

1: A Little Light Shines

When I was about five years old, Mamma and I took a trip on the train. She dressed me in my favorite outfit, a yellow taffeta dress with ruffles on the bottom, and she tied matching bows to my freshly braided hair. Oh, I was so happy, all "gussied up" and tingling with excitement while shining with pride and joy! I do not know what sparkled the most: my petroleum jelly-coated face or my freshly polished black patent leather shoes. I really liked those pretty little shoes, too! So many times, while I was sitting down, I stretched my little legs straight in front of me and gazed into the top of my shoes. I smiled while looking for my reflection. It is amazing, the quirky things that can fascinate a child.

It was a sweltering, hot summer day when we arrived at the train station and the fumes from the diesel engines of the huge locomotives smelled like rotten eggs and filled the air. The extreme heat plus the handful of grapes that I had eaten from our packed lunch upset my stomach. Those perfectly polished shoes did not stay pretty very long. After we entered the huge wooden doors that opened into the train station, portions from our packed lunch came up with specks of the recently eaten red grapes. Fortunately, none of it got on my pretty yellow dress but some of the "upchuck" did cover the toes of those shiny black patent leather shoes, all to my dismay.

My mother quickly responded to the miniature disaster by removing my now mucky shoes and telling me to stay put and watch the luggage as she headed to the bathroom to remove the smelly mess. Later she returned to the location only to find two suitcases in the place where she had left me, and I was nowhere nearby. After what probably felt like an exhaustive search for her, she found me sitting on a bench surrounded by several people. I imagine I was swinging my little legs and feet in the yellow socks with dirty bottoms by now as I chatted with my newly discovered audience. Happily, I sat looking like a caramel-colored version of "Little Miss Susie Sunshine." Even as a child, I enjoyed the lively art of conversation and used it fully every opportunity I could. There were no strangers in my life.

Mamma walked over to me and smiled as she reached for my hand and guided me away while handing me my freshly cleaned shoes. I quickly responded, "thank you, but Mamma, I was just telling all of the nice folks ...."

Without saying a word, she continued to hold my hand and marched me to the "right" section of the train station, the one labeled **COLORED.** As we walked away, I turned and waved to the group of white acquaintances and said, "bye, bye y'all," and they responded with smiles and waves in return.

As a child of such a young age, I was not aware of the legal consequences of racial mixing in public places during that era in the United States of America. Understandably, I did not know the repercussions that a person could suffer from public interracial assembly. It was much later that I realized, as a friendly child, I might have been accepted among a group of pleasant white passengers, but Mamma was well aware of the fact that she may not have been. My mother simply corrected my naive transgression in a wise manner by leading me away.

During that era of Jim Crow laws, "separate and unequal" in Alabama and all of the surrounding states in the South, the consequences were extremely severe for such violations. On that particular day, the dreadful penalties for such laws were temporarily suspended. God shined a light on this amiable little "colored girl," as I was called during that era, to allow the incident to peacefully blend into the hearts of a handful of southern white citizens. I believe there was genuine warmth in the hearts and smiles among those people.

That was only one of the many journeys that Miss Grace and I experienced on our mother-daughter

Traveling Down the Road With Grace

journeys while traveling across the country. As a child, it seemed that my Mamma was not afraid to go anywhere, and her actions always made me feel so courageous and brave. That time during the 1950s was not the safest era, especially in the South, for a Black lady travelling with her young child.

Frequently, Mamma packed a lunch and a suitcase or two and after we were dressed, off we would go on the train or bus to visit Daddy, who was in the Army. Later I learned that he had personal battles. After returning home from the war, my father fought demons with bottles of alcohol which later led to the separation from his wife and young daughter.

Travelling was a well-defined setting for the stage of segregation in the United States of America with obvious signs of distinction between the Black and white races. I remember **the changing of seats** after the train or bus crossed the Mason-Dixon line. So many of the colored travelers remained in the back seats either from weariness of traveling or just pure convenience, but not my Mamma! Staying in the back was not an option when it was not required. Without saying a word, she took my hand and guided me to the "right" section of the train or bus, while sitting as near to the front as possible and always giving me the window seat to look out and see the world that we were passing through. What a strange world it appeared to be! The same people, the same vehicle, the same country, and we had to sit in the back in the South, but we could sit in the front in the North. As a child I wondered, "why .... why?"

When I matured, I learned about Jim Crow laws and how to adhere to the rules of racial segregation in the South. It was later in life when I discovered the unspoken rules had changed up North to **James Crow** laws, just as poignant and ever so present with the unwritten signs for the **colored** public bathrooms and the water fountains that were easily recognized by being unclean.

Years later, as a student at the university, I joined my fellow Black and white students when we marched and protested the humongous repercussions of all of the racial discrimination that had swelled and spread so rapidly through our country like a contagious disease. When I learned of the blood being spilled throughout our nation in the name of equality, my thoughts returned to the day when the little girl in the yellow dress was sitting on a bench, talking with her newfound "friends" in a segregated train station in rural Alabama. That could have been a dangerous situation, and it **was** for so many young Black boys and girls and men and women.

Thank God, He let a little light shine on the little girl in the yellow dress.

Traveling Down the Road With Grace

2: Imprints In The Dirt

Every story needs a pillar of strength, and in my life, that was Miss Lillian—my formidable grandmother who taught us resilience in every sweeping motion." I called her "Big Mamma," and she was a big woman in every sense of the word, weight-wise and otherwise. She had a significant influence on all of our lives!

Besides being a mother of sixteen children, she was also blessed with more than double that number of grandchildren. Although the lady could be very tough sometimes, she was also tender and compassionate, especially with us younger ones. I always knew that Big Mamma's love and concern for our family was limitless and there was never a shortage of love in her heart or in our home.

When I was a little girl, I thought my grandmother was the best cook in the world! When I grew older, I knew, without a doubt, that she was the best cook in my world! Even her cornbread was sumptuous, and sometimes I thought, "If she put some icing on that bread, it would look just like a delicious cake." Of course, she would never do such a foolhardy thing because it tastes as good as cornbread! Besides, her cakes were the absolute best and I refuse to talk about her delicious pastries! Nor will I reveal a single word describing her peach cobblers, sweet potato pies, tea cakes, and gingerbread. My words cannot describe them, but after a few bites, all I could say was, "**MMM-MMMM!**"

She raised hens and chickens, and they produced an abundant supply of eggs for her baking needs and also served as an addition to our breakfasts. Sometimes, a few of those plump and tender "yardbirds" were sacrificed, and we received a delicious treat! They became golden when she fried a few and filled a large platter that was placed in the middle of the table on Sundays for our supper.

In addition to being an awesome cook, Big Mamma was a Law Enforcer! She made the laws, and we followed them to the letter. Her weapon of choice was a switch! In case you are not familiar with that particular item, it is supposed to be a small twig used to lightly tap a child's legs or bottom for punishment.

When Big Mamma needed a replacement weapon, she simply pulled down the entire tree limb, and the lady did not tap gently either! She did not play fair. To tell the truth, my grandmother did not play at all. I do not believe Child Protective Services existed in rural Alabama in the 1950s, and if they did, they were afraid to come to our home.

In the country, everyone wakes up with the chickens, if not before. That big, old rooster starts crowing before daybreak, and we climb out of our beds, wash up in a tin basin, get dressed, and have breakfast, which is usually hot-baked biscuits with syrup and butter. Sometimes eggs are fried on the large wood-burning stove, depending on how productive her hens were that week.

Afterward, all of her grandchildren "went to work!" During the summertime, Big Mamma made all of the little folks sweep the dirt in the yard with her homemade straw brooms every day, except on Sundays and when it was raining. The younger children thought it was fun and made a game out of the chore. We older ones thought it was senseless and borderline insane, although we never shared those thoughts with her.

If the temperatures were 19 or 99 degrees, we swept the dirt almost every day! We obeyed her commands without a complaint or gripe, at least not within her hearing range. By obeying Big Mamma's instructions, we eventually learned how to create perfectly formed grooves in the red dirt as we produced an immaculately groomed yard. After all, we were taught by a master teacher!

Later in life, I realized that while we made imprints in the dirt, Big Mamma imprinted strong and effective work ethics in our lives. As a result of her rigorous training sessions, her grandchildren advanced from her yard with the ability to become employed and remain industrious workers.

Years later, a friend and I were sharing our childhood experiences, and I told her about Big Mamma's dirt-sweeping sessions. My colleague had lived all her younger years up North in a neighborhood bordered by concrete sidewalks and grassy-covered lawns, and she had never heard of people sweeping dirt. After I told her about my childhood lessons, we wondered where the idea of sweeping dirt originated.

Out of curiosity, we researched the practice and discovered that the tradition originated in West Africa. The idea was brought to America via slavery, like so many traditions that our people still practice today. It is believed that the notion of sweeping yards grew out of necessity. Some people thought sweeping dirt was conceived when yards became an extension of the home and certain areas served as outdoor rooms. According to our research, sweeping yards was common because of the heat and space constraints. In some parts of the world, most family gatherings, such as cooking and washing clothes, take place in the yards outside of the home.

I remembered my grandmother's big iron wash pot in her yard, and Mondays were always "wash days." Also, there were clotheslines nearby to hang the freshly washed laundry to dry, and the damp clothes were hung using clothespins in a tight, straight form to eliminate wrinkles.

"Wow!" I thought as I began to connect the dots. Since yards were used as workstations, sweeping the yards developed as a form of pest control and safety surrounding the homes. With the elimination of grass, there was no place for pesty insects and snakes to hide. Because of the hot weather, outdoor cooking and laundering became standard practices in the yards that had been swept. There was less chance of fire with cinders igniting dry grass.

In today's modern times, there are people who still sweep dirt in several countries. Years ago, I traveled to Ghana and West Africa and visited areas of that country that reminded me of my hometown in southern Alabama, which has a similar climate and terrain. I smiled when the tour bus drove through the countryside, and we saw a handful of children and a few women sweeping dirt. Yes, and it was red dirt, too, just like in Alabama! Suddenly, I felt a genuine "connection" with the people there. . . . . . . and I said to myself, "Yes, my people!"

3: Summertime, Good Times

Mamma took me to Alabama for the summer after she and my father separated. This was a bittersweet time because I missed my Daddy, but I liked the peace and enjoyment of living with Big Mamma. She made all of her grandchildren feel so special and being her first grandchild was a badge of honor I proudly wore.

The other grandchildren were residents of this little country town that we loved so much while I was a "summer drop-off." Regardless of my status, I enjoyed "the resort," a big, old country house with several rooms and a long porch on one side. Our house sat on red dirt, down a red, dusty road that was so ingeniously named Red Road.

Granddaddy was a contractor and a bricklayer. Not only did he build "the resort," the big dwelling for his extremely large family, but he also constructed the two nearby homes, that he rented to other families. The income from his rental property and the salary he received from his full-time job provided for his wife and their sixteen children, who progressively became "grown and gone" and the batch of grandchildren under their custodial care from time to time.

This hard-working man took time on Saturday afternoons to load all of the little folks, his grandchildren, in the back of his shiny, black Ford truck, which he had meticulously washed and polished. He drove us to town for ice cream and treats. On Sunday mornings, we piled in the back of the truck again, and this time, we headed in the opposite direction to the little country church down the road.

As an only child, I was delighted to have a constant playmate, my little auntie, Marcie, who is three years younger than I am. My grandparent's youngest child was one tough little cookie. She was also my petite partner in crime, and I just loved her! The two of us would roam and play throughout the countryside and sometimes we got into a little ruckus with the bunch of kids who lived across the road. Most of the time, I got us into trouble, and Marcie fought us out of the mischief, and she always won, too!

Living in southern Alabama was a little bit of heaven on earth when I was growing up. We had so much fun running and playing barefoot in the yard and chasing the chickens under the house. Big Mamma had a cow named Shirley, whose tail we always tried to pull while the heifer swatted the flies off her rump. It was amazing, all of the quirky little things that can fascinate a child.

The nearby wooded areas offered loads of exploration, with so many of Mother Nature's wildlife lessons waiting for us to discover and learn. That neighboring region was an inquisitive youngster's playground. Lots of pine trees filled the woods, and an assortment of beautiful wild flowers flourished near the surrounding creek. There, we discovered a variety of birds, frogs, lizards, snakes, butterflies, and even a few unknown critters. Country life was wonderful, especially if you were a child and had many cousins, a little auntie as your constant playmate, a caring Big Mamma, and a Granddaddy to love on all of you.

4: Adoption In The Family

The air buzzed with anticipation as the house transformed under Big Mamma's diligent hands, signaling the arrival of *"company"*—a change that would shape my life forever. Yes, Big Mamma's oldest brother and his wife finally arrived all the way from Gary, Indiana. As the last days of summer appeared, so did a long, sleek, black Oldsmobile 88 sedan coming down the country road, kicking up clouds of red dust behind it.

For the first time, I met my great-uncle and his wife. When I looked at the lovely lady, she smiled at me, and I grinned back at her. Immediately, we were in love and wanted to stay together. For that to happen, the grown folks had to obtain my mother's permission for such a significant transformation to occur. My aunt and uncle spent the next week in our little country town while my grandfather contacted Mamma and made an agreement. With a handful of stipulations, my mother gave me permission to live with my aunt and uncle.

On the day we left, tears started to swell in my eyes when I said goodbye to my grandparents and little auntie. I knew I would miss them and was sad to leave, but I also felt courageous. Mamma had taught me that. There were many great and wonderful experiences "up North!"

When it was time for us to leave, I was so excited and eager to discover all the adventures with my new parents. I climbed into the back seat of their car and sat as straight as possible with my legs crossed at the ankles and imagined myself a young princess. I started to wave and smile at the travelers in the cars driving by. Surprisingly, many of them smiled and waved back at me! I turned my head from side to side to see the passing scenes as we were traveling on the highways while riding through little country towns and large metropolitan cities. Quickly, I learned that pretending to be a princess was hard work. All that, sitting up straight and crossing my legs was not comfortable, especially since I had never done that before. I got tired and rested between the "sitting" sessions. "Even a princess needs to relax and take a little nap."

I noticed the scenery was changing from the rural backgrounds with farmlands and tiny houses on dirt roads to big and tall brick buildings stacked along the paved streets. When we rode through the large cities, I saw grass growing in the yards and pretty flowers blooming around the houses. "The children who live in those houses don't have to sweep the dirt in their yards like we did at Big Mamma's house. I hope the home with my aunt and uncle will have grass in the yard," I thought to myself, but I did not say anything because I knew I would be happy even if it did not.

My aunt told me the names of the states and the big cities as we rode through them. She taught me lessons, and I wanted to learn as much as I could. Although these were strange and unfamiliar places that we were passing through, I tried hard to remember the names.

Finally, their long, black car stopped, and when I looked out of the window, I saw a large two-story home. The front yard had grass growing with pretty bushes and beautiful flowers. Of course, I was excited and happy when I realized I had arrived at our new home with my new parents, my aunt and uncle.

While growing up, I was blessed to have two mothers: one young and the other elderly. I became a youthful woman with an old soul. Later in life, I learned that this arrangement of informal adoption was not unusual. Sometimes, when a young mother has a child, older family members raise the youngster. This situation is most likely if the older relatives are childless. My mother was a teenager when I was born, and my aunt and uncle were elderly when I came into their lives.

There were no court actions or legal adoption procedures. I simply left one family member's home and moved into another one, and the transaction was completed with the transfer of a suitcase. The procedure was considered legal and proper, and the process was sealed with love and family acceptance. My new parents had to acquire a copy of my birth certificate in order to enroll me in school, and classes started shortly after our arrival.

Although my mother and I did not live together all of the time, she was always in my life. During the summer months, I stayed with her when I was out of school, and she visited us for Christmas holidays and special occasions. Mamma mailed gifts and large boxes of beautiful clothes for my birthdays and during the year. I always knew the decision she made was for my enhancement and I was a happy, well-adjusted child with a fulfilled and wonderful life.

My aunt introduced me to music when she exposed me to concerts and recitals. My uncle purchased a brand-new piano for me, and I had weekly piano lessons with a professional music instructor. Both of my new parents placed a strong emphasis on academic achievement, and they did all they could to enhance my education. I remember they also bought a set of World Book Encyclopedia on a monthly payment plan. My uncle was a steel mill worker, and my aunt did housecleaning for "well-to-do families."

It appeared interesting to me that my aunt and I physically resembled each other. Frequently, I wondered if this was "coincidence or providence?" Both of us had the same-colored eyes. Our skin tones were identical, and we even had similar body structures. Occasionally, people who did not know our history, thought she was my natural mother and had birthed me later in her life.

Growing up in the home of the Chairman of the Deacon Board of a Baptist church contributed greatly to the development of my spiritual life. At a young age, I had a personal relationship with God and was very familiar with the Bible, thanks to the religious training from my new parents, along with regular church attendance, Sunday School, and B.T.U.

This transition was a major change in my life, and I believe it was God's plan. My aunt and uncle raised me as their child from the age of seven years old to adulthood. During my younger years, I may have picked a few wildflowers along the way, but I never wandered so far that I could not find the pathway back home. Thank God!

5: Time

"Where have all of the years gone?" This is a question I frequently ask myself as time seems to pass more rapidly since I have grown older. So many of my family members have departed this earth and I certainly miss them. My elderly aunt and uncle left decades ago, and soon afterward, Big Mamma passed, and a few years later, Granddaddy followed her. Twelve of my mother's siblings departed this world within a few decades. Our hearts were sharply pierced when the youngest daughter, Marcie, passed away at such a young and tender age. Shortly afterward, my grandparent's large family of sixteen children diminished to only four remaining siblings: my mother, two younger sisters, and their youngest brother.

Throughout the years, I have learned that when you really love someone, they may not be physically present in your life anymore, but they are never gone. God preserves our love for them in our hearts forever, and they are always a memory and a heartbeat away.

Traveling Down the Road With Grace

There is a Time for Everything

There is an occasion for everything,
and a time for every activity under heaven.
A time to give birth and a time to die,
a time to plant and a time to uproot.
A time to kill and a time to heal.
A time to tear down and a time to build.
A time to weep and a time to laugh.
A time to mourn and a time to dance.
A time to throw stones and a time to gather stones.
A time to embrace and a time to avoid embracing,
time to search and a time to count as lost,
a time to keep and a time to throw away.
A time to tear and a time to sew.
A time to be silent and a time to speak.
A time to love and a time to hate.
A time for war and a time for peace.

ECCLESIASTES 3:1-8

6: New Orleans

The longing to reconnect with my roots drew me back home to Alabama, but it was the promise of adventure that took Mamma and me to the vibrant streets of New Orleans. I decided to "go home," the little town in southern Alabama where I was born and the place where my mother currently lives. Just thinking about that place warms my heart and makes me smile.

After I arrived, Mamma and I lingered around the house for a few days, and afterward, we decided to take a road trip together. We talked about possible places to visit and decided on the city of New Orleans, Louisiana. We packed our bags, drove onto the highway, and headed down Interstate I-65.

Years ago, I saw the movie, *Walk on the Wild Side*, which was set in New Orleans. The leading star of the film was an attractive lady named Capucine. The movie depicted the city as such an intriguing place, and I always wanted to travel there one day. Although I was a teenager when I saw the movie, I never lost my desire to visit New Orleans and the surrounding Louisiana Bayou. This year, my mother and I left Alabama to explore that fascinating place.

Our arrival in the city was somewhat delayed. During Mamma's younger years, back in the day, she enjoyed the "CLING, CLING" sounds of the casinos as they spread throughout the country. When my mother saw all of the bright lights and neon signs flashing from Tunica, Mississippi, she immediately wanted to stop, and we did. We visited those "one-armed bandits," and a few hours later, with her pocketbook a little lighter, we crossed Lake Pontchartrain and arrived in New Orleans, the city named after the Duke of Orleans.

We had dinner at Antoine's, where we enjoyed our first dinner in New Orleans at one of the finest restaurants in the city. The next few days, we walked down the famous Bourbon Street and discovered even more extraordinary restaurants where we savored plenty of fresh oysters and boiled crawfish. Each day was a culinary adventure when we found even more delicacies and had our share of gumbo, jambalaya, and etouffee. Our meals included one of our favorite side dishes, red beans and rice, which we later learned was also a delightful dish for one of New Orleans' native sons, Mr. Louis Armstrong. Legend has it he regularly signed his letters, "Red beans and Ricely yours."

We dined exceptionally well and even made acquaintances with a couple of the local culinary celebrities. We met Chef Paul Prudhomme while he was working at his famous restaurant, K-Paul's Louisiana Kitchen. One evening, my mother and I searched for more outstanding culinary delicacies, and we discovered the exceptional hostess and cook, Mrs. Leah Chase. The energetic lady was in her eighties and still meeting and greeting guests at her family's world-famous restaurant, Dooky Chase's, and she graciously signed a copy of her famous cookbook for us.

Our favorite discovery was the famous Café du Monde. This open-air coffee shop is unique and well-known for its café au lait and beignets, which have been made and served there continuously since 1862. The famous eatery is located on Decatur Street and is open 24 hours every day of the year except Christmas and during the hurricane seasons. Riding the city's streetcars and trollies was an excellent way to explore the historic areas such as the Garden District and New_Orleans_neighborhoods" neighborhood French Quarter.

The tour of the buildings in this area was an extraordinary display of the city's beautiful architecture. We saw creative metalwork patterns in the iron fences and the picturesque stained glass designs on some of the exquisite churches.

We enjoyed the melodious street musicians when they belted out their distinctive sounds of the

"New Orleans style jazz" while we walked throughout the city. I smiled when I watched my mother begin to sway with the rhythm of the music and later danced a few steps. It was so obvious she was having a great time in "N'awlin's!" While the children were dancing for dollars, the musicians were playing their instruments and singing in perfect harmony on some of the street corners. The sounds of the New Orleans-style music filled the air. This coastal city, which straddles the Mississippi River, is so unique. We had a wonderful time in NOLA!

7. The Sunshine State.

Thanksgiving in Alabama has always been a comforting tradition, but this time, a spontaneous road trip to the Sunshine State brought unexpected surprises and gratification. Mamma and I prepared the traditional turkey holiday dinner with all the trimmings. A few days later, we were "stuffed" with turkey and tired of football. We decided to visit the Sunshine State, Florida, for a change of scenery.

Since we did not have a scheduled arrival time, we leisurely rode along the highway and stopped by every T. J. Maxx store along the route. What should have been a trip of merely a few hours became an extremely long day's journey. Ultimately, we reached our final destination. We were a bit tired but extremely delighted and loaded with lots of TJM bags that filled the trunk of the car. We had the pleasure of thoroughly enjoying a trip not strictly planned with definite details but with lots of pleasant and relaxing time together.

Getting off the beaten path and enjoying the scenery and shopping felt good. Frequently, travel agendas are very tightly planned, and travelers do not enjoy their journey because their schedules are too rigid. Not so with this trip. We enjoyed every mile of our journey while riding down the roads that led us to all of those Maxx stores, where we obtained plenty of "store-bought happiness."

Once we arrived in Orlando, the city in the center of the Sunshine State, we visited the home of Disney's most famous mouse, and there we discovered the EPCOT Center, where we explored for a while as we wandered through the exhibits of various countries. While we walked through the area, I wondered, "Now, why did we come here?" Everyone knows that Disney Parks are specifically designed to delight children, which may please their parents and grandparents, but not **two elderly ladies who arrived without kids**!

After a short while at the celebrated theme park, I had another "what was I thinking?" moment. Mom said very little, as usual, but a big smile appeared across her face when I suggested, "Let's go," and we quickly departed Mr. Disney's place. Later, I had to admit, I only wanted to visit the theme park so we would be able to say, "We went to Disney World!" and we said it, too, while searching for the nearest exit out of town, and we quickly left Orlando!

We arrived in St. Augustine, Florida, and spotted a large sign that pointed to Ponce de Leon's Fountain of Youth. "Now, this may be a great place for two elderly ladies to visit," I jokingly said to Miss

Traveling Down the Road With Grace

Grace. She smiled at me while shaking her head and responded, "Girl, just go wherever you want to go. It is alright with me." My mother is the most agreeable and easygoing person I know.

I followed the directions on the signs, and after a few twists and turns and turning around again, we finally reached the location. We stopped and leisurely wandered throughout the area for a while. Neither of us was impressed with the location, so we left after a brief stroll around the area. As we were returning to the car, I whispered to my mother, "Perhaps we did not stay long enough to become youthful-looking again." She chuckled and responded, "We could stay there as long as you want, and we will still look the same!" I smiled and shook my head in total agreement. My mother has always had a delightful sense of humor. She is witty and wise; the older I become, the more I appreciate her sage wisdom.

We drove further and passed a bookstore in the center of St. Augustine, Florida, which, by the way, is one of the oldest cities in the United States. Of course, we stopped and browsed through the enormous assortment of books. The bookseller who greeted us told us about an extremely bizarre incident that occurred in another Floridian town.

"The horrible confrontation occurred previously in a local Black town that had disappeared," she informed us. "Oh no!" I exclaimed as I wondered, "How could such a tragedy happen?" My mother and I were curious after hearing bits and pieces of the story, and we both wanted to learn more details about this unbelievable incident, and we did.

We purchased a copy of the book, and the author revealed the actual account of the little-known incident that occurred in a small, Black Floridian town that was completely destroyed. All of its inhabitants were killed by angry whites on New Year's Day in 1923! The African American residents living in this particular location were very wealthy middle-class entrepreneurs and landowners. The devastation lasted for several days when an enraged white mob brutally annihilated the affluent and well-established community. We left the bookstore with a copy of the newly discovered book, **"LIKE JUDGEMENT DAY, The Ruin and Redemption of a Town** Called **Rosewood."**

After we returned home, a visit to our neighborhood library led us to additional information about this particular dreadful massacre in American history. Unfortunately, we also learned about even more devastating confrontations that happened across America in the South, North, East, and West. Traveling revealed lessons about our country that were not included in the history classes in my school books!

Reading books that reflected our travels became a practice after the trip to St. Augustine, Florida. Later, as we continued to travel to different parts of the country, this became a custom that we have maintained throughout our years of traveling. Reading and collecting books related to our trips proved to be tremendously beneficial for us later in our lives.

Some evenings, I open one of our "travel books," and Mom and I *return* to one of our previous trips using the related book. I read segments from the book aloud as she turns the pages, and we discuss bits of the information and the pictures. I believe my mother's recognition of the photographs and our discussions about the topics helped her memory and mine. Also, this is a bonus blessing for us since it is an enjoyable way to enhance quality mother-daughter time together. Mamma and I have discovered that frequently sharing information from the numerous books about the places we visit is beneficial for us. We expand our horizons, share quality time together, and learn more about interesting places.

8: Grace Was At The Wedding

As the dawn of a new millennium unfolded, so did one of the most memorable chapters of my life—a wedding that would bring love, courage, and, of course, Grace to center stage. A person unaware would have thought it was my first marriage with all of the excitement surrounding this special event. The destination wedding was held in June on the beautiful tropical island nation of Montego Bay, Jamaica.

My mother, brave as she is, traveled solo from Alabama to Jamaica. Knowing that international travel is not for the weak and faint-hearted, I marveled at her courage. She seemed to have discovered an extra dose of bravery, which she actually needed.

During the wedding rehearsal, the day before the event, my son told me that he received a telephone call from an airport official in Miami, Florida, who informed him that Mamma had been in an accident. The officer told him that his grandmother fell when she was boarding the plane and was taken to a nearby hospital in an ambulance. That was all we knew about the incident and our attempts to get additional information failed. We repeatedly called the airport and the hospital throughout the remainder of the day and well into late evening.

Early the next morning, we finally heard from Mamma. She called to tell us she had arrived at the airport in Montego Bay and wanted to know who would pick her up. Immediately, her grandson left to get her. When my mother arrived at the hotel, she told us that she never went to the hospital although she was advised to go. She also said that she experienced some pain from the fall but refused to let it slow her down and, least of all, prevent her from attending her daughter's wedding. The lady did everything she could to board the next plane headed in our direction in order to arrive on time and she did! Yes, my mother arrived at the special occasion!

This was merely one of many circumstances when Mamma exhibited extraordinary strength and fortitude. In fact, she displayed such qualities so frequently that they became second nature to her. I consider her amazing and am blessed to have such a role model. With determination and perseverance, my mother arrived at my wedding. Of all the guests who attended the ceremony, I believe she was the happiest and most proud.

Yes, Queen Grace, as I think of her, stood so elegant and regal. On that afternoon in June, in the picturesque wedding garden in Montego Bay, surrounded with lovely tropical flowers, magnificent trees, and attractive guests, my son escorted me down the aisle to stand next to my tall and handsome groom as we exchanged our sacred vows to love and cherish each other. All of the wedding guests looked gorgeous, dressed in their all-white attire, a Jamaican tradition! I was so happy to marry in the midst of God's beauty and love, and Grace was at my wedding.

9: Saved By Grace

The joy of taking my granddaughter, Michelle Grace, on her first airplane ride marked a new generation's journey through the cherished paths of my childhood. We headed to Alabama during the summer and spent a week with my mother. This was the place where I enjoyed some of the best portions of my childhood, and I hope Michelle will gather memories and moments that will become significant for her as the two Graces spend time together.

During our flight, I thought about the times I was a little girl traveling with my mother many years ago. Michelle and I will not change seats after crossing the Mason-Dixon line, like my mother and I did decades ago. Many things have changed in our world today, but not all. Thanks to the powerful Civil Rights movement that swept our country during the 1960s, many doors have opened for people of color, but there are still mountains to climb. Like all parents, we hope for a better future for our children.

Once *Little Mack*, as I affectionately called her, and I arrived in that small country town, we spent time relaxing and enjoying the scenery and slow-paced atmosphere of the countryside. My mother and I relaxed on the shaded front porch as we sipped fresh

Traveling Down the Road With Grace

lemonade loaded with ice while catching up on the latest news about our family members and neighbors. Little Mack played nearby as she sat splashing the water in her inflatable swimming pool, placed under the large, shade trees in the yard. After a few hours of chatting and watching the occasional vehicles pass down the road, Mamma suggested we go shopping, and the three of us readily headed to the shopping mall in the nearby city.

While browsing through the aisles, we separated. After a bit of time passed, Mamma walked next to me and asked if Michelle was with me. "No!" I quickly responded, "I thought she was with you!" Immediately, we started calling her name while searching for her throughout the store. "Where could that little girl be?" We wondered while we anxiously searched the surrounding areas of the store.

Soon, a few concerned fellow shoppers joined us in our pursuit after we described what she was wearing and how tall she stood. I was trying not to get upset as I prayed we would find her soon. A newly formed search party member suggested we contact security and have her paged. While quickly heading in that direction, I passed the ladies' restroom, and automatically stopped to open the door. Surprised but very happy to see her, there stood Mack! I recognized her from her back since she was standing at the sink.

Traveling Down the Road With Grace

After taking a deep breath while trying to calm myself, I questioned her, "Michelle, where have you been? What are you doing?" She immediately turned around with a big smile on her face as she held out her wet, soapy hands towards me and responded, "Look, Grandma! I'm washing my hands, **too, as** you told me always to do!"

With an enormous sigh of relief plus a resounding, "Thank You, Jesus!" I hurried to dry her hands and take her out of the restroom. As soon as I spotted my mother with a few members of the 'Search Party,' I joyfully announced, "Here she is! I found her!" The small group heartily cheered and clapped as Michelle burst into a wide grin. She did not know the cause of all the commotion nor what the small crowd that started to surround her was about, but she joyfully joined the celebration as she continued to smile and clap her hands while standing in the middle of the small group of volunteers who continued to enthusiastically cheer as they encircled her.

Indeed, I was relieved but upset! "This little girl did not have the slightest idea what we had gone through," I thought to myself. Just as I was about to scold her, Mamma stepped between us and placed her arms around Michelle's little shoulders as she started to gently massage her back while comforting her. Then my mother looked at me and said, "I'm sure she won't do it again. We will talk to her and besides, we really should have been paying more attention and watching her more carefully." The smiling great-grandmother continued to gently massage her little great-grand girl's back as she tenderly hugged her. "Yes," I thought to myself, "my mother is right."

What a heart-warming sight they were: the wise and elderly great-grandmother, bending down and hugging her "Little Mack," the nickname we have given Michele since her birth. Mamma calmly reassured the child that everything was all right while continuing to gently massage her back. The tenderness of that moment started to melt all of my anxieties away. Softly, I whispered again, "Thank you, Lord! Thank you for watching over our little girl and keeping her safe!"

When Great Grace, the affectionate nickname that Michelle has called her great-grandmother since she could clearly speak, reached for the little girl's freshly washed hand to lead her out the door, I remembered, . . . Yes!

Suddenly the memory flashed in my mind when Mamma reached for my hand to lead me away. That incident occurred so many years ago. It was decades ago when I was the little girl who wandered away at the train station! That happened so long ago, I had almost forgotten, but now, seeing Mack and my mother together today, reminded me of how I felt when Mamma firmly held my hand. She always made me feel so courageous and brave! I smiled at them as I began to realize that, now Michelle Grace will feel that way, also, as another little girl is . . . . SAVED BY GRACE!

10: Home In Alabama

Time passed, and the days turned into weeks, then months. Although we talked on the phone every day, I realized I had not seen my mother in a while. I was missing her and decided to check on flights to Alabama and thankfully, I found a reasonable fare. "Well, why not?" I thought to myself and quickly decided to purchase a ticket, hop on a plane, and spend some time with Mamma. I also remembered the relaxing pleasures of the massages and manicures that we recently discovered in her little town.

A few days later, I was on an airplane headed to Alabama, and when I arrived at my mother's home, I was utterly shocked! It was challenging to understand the extreme changes that had occurred in such a short time, and I was unprepared for what I discovered. "It was just a few months ago when Michelle and I visited Mamma, and she was fine!" I repeatedly reminded myself. I was in total disbelief when I saw her and the environment that my mother was living in!

It was difficult to understand how the situation had changed so drastically in such a short time. Mamma and I talked to each other every day! Sometimes we were on the phone two or three times daily and I **always** asked, "Mamma, how are you doing?" I inquired about my stepfather, and she

Traveling Down the Road With Grace

responded, "Oh Baby, everybody is just fine," and I believed her.

I was stunned when I arrived and discovered the situation that my mother was currently living in. It was a DISASTER! Her world seemed to have tumbled and CRASHED, and she appeared to be trapped under the demolition while trying to survive! My mother had problems getting her medications as well as remembering to take them. Her meals were sporadic and unhealthy. She missed her regularly scheduled doctors' appointments. If that was not bad enough, to make matters worse, my stepfather's health had deteriorated, and his current battle with cancer had intensified. It seemed as though family support was ambiguous!

What was initially planned as a delightful social visit to my mother's home turned into a decision for her to return home with me. Her current living situation was critical, and in order for her to survive, I knew significant changes had to be made immediately! I checked into a nearby hotel since I could not stay at the family home because the situation was so volatile.

Feeling desperate for solutions, I prayed. Early the next morning, God revealed the plan for us to follow. When I opened the Gideon Bible located in the desk drawer in the hotel room, the scripture revealed:

"for the battle is not yours, but God's." II Chronicles 20:15.

The Master was true to His Word. The scriptures that I read began a new journey. After arranging flights for us to return home, the rest of the story grew into additional chapters of our revised journey as a mother-daughter team. We sought "the one who has the Key of David," "what He opens no one can shut, and what He shuts no one can open," Revelation 3:7.

We gathered some of my mother's personal belongings in the same timeframe as Jehoshaphat prepared to exit in the scriptures, II Chronicles 20:25, which said, "They found much among them, including goods, garments, and valuable things which they took for themselves more than they could carry. And they were three days taking the spoils because there was so much." God's Word is true!

For three days, we were packing my mother's possessions and, yes, I also discovered an abundance of valuable jewelry and large amounts of money but the most precious of all the valuables was Mamma! Monday arrived, and we boarded an early morning flight. I knew that as the plane was taxiing down the runway, she would never return to the situation that God had delivered her from. While my mother and I were traveling to my home in Denver, Colorado, one thought reverberated in my mind, "she cradled me in her arms when I was young; now it is my turn to care for her since she has grown older." When our flight landed and we arrived at my hometown, I was totally committed to giving my mother the best that I could offer her. With God's help, I knew we would make it.

As time passed, Mamma began to adjust to her new life. God closed doors from her past and opened new doors for her future as she peacefully accepted the finality of her previous life in Alabama. Eventually, Mamma began to acquire a comfortable lifestyle as her health gradually improved and she started to look more like her former self, attractive and wholesome.

We gradually experienced more progressive changes as God led us on our new journey. He picked us up and guided us and we continued to move in new directions. The turning point occurred when we looked upward instead of outward. We started our days with prayer and God's Word. Mamma has always possessed a heart of love, and her life has been a reflection of that love. I prayed that she would maintain segments of sweetness from her previous years and keep the good portions in her heart, along with her love and memories of her husband, who later passed away.

11: Another Family Adoption

Mamma and I were living in Denver, Colorado, when my ***goddaughter, Aundria, visited us. She met my mother for the first time. Both of them were looking forward to meeting and spending some quality time together, and they did! After dinner, Mamma and Aundria connected and bonded when they washed and dried the dishes together. This newly formed "Grandma/Granddaughter" duo*** continued their nonstop conversation that lasted well into the night. I left the two chatterboxes in the living room and went to bed.

The next morning while I was preparing breakfast, I overheard Aundria say, "Good Morning, Grandma," and my mother instantly responded, "Hi, Baby! How are you feeling this morning?" As I continued to scramble the eggs and check the toast, it was obvious that Aundria and my mother had become connected and were extremely fond of each other. Aundria had found a grandmother, and my mother has remained connected with her newly discovered granddaughter, and they have been loving each other since.

A few years later, Aundria relocated to Austin, Texas and Mamma and I were living in Dallas, Texas. Summer was fading and autumn was beginning to appear, and we started to think about our traditional fall foliage tour.

"Let's go to Austin this year," I suggested to my mother, and she responded, "Okay, if you want to!" We decided to visit Austin, Texas, which happens to be the capital of the Lone Star state and the current hometown of my mother's adult granddaughter.

I purchased two airplane tickets and called my goddaughter to give her our ETA. We had a pleasant flight and arrived on time but as we were leaving the airfield, I saw a very peculiar sight! It was such an extraordinary display of unassuming country charm near the Bergstrom Austin Airport. Located at the nearby exit, directly across the road, we saw a small herd of spectacular longhorn cattle! The flock was grazing in a field near the airport, and they appeared as content as a cluster of cows could be. There were no written signs nor billboards near the scene, but the message was clear and well-defined, **Welcome** to **Austin, Texas!**

Aundrea was waiting for us when we arrived at the terminal, and she helped us get our luggage. Afterward, she took two very hungry ladies to a restaurant for their first meal in Austin. Once we were seated, she automatically ordered lunch for her grandmother and herself. Of course, I wondered, "How did she know chicken enchiladas are Mamma's favorite Mexican meal?" I never told her, and Mom had not said a word either. When I asked how she knew, she just smiled at me and smugly replied, "Oh, I know, I know what Grandma likes!" "Well," I had to admit, "It seems as though you do," I responded with a smile. Mamma just looked at both of us while she started to eat her enchiladas.

Aundria and her grandmother continued to grin at each other. Although Mamma did not say much, as usual, her eyes and smiles let us know that she was enjoying all of the attention she was receiving. I never realized my mother enjoyed Mexican food so much! The cheerful camaraderie and the delicious food combined made everything so enjoyable for the three of us.

The next day, a pleasant Saturday afternoon, we were riding around town sightseeing and enjoying the scenery when suddenly we approached an unexpected bonus of the day: a Saturday afternoon college football game! When we passed the stadium, we saw all of the cheering fans packed in the stands, and we had the opportunity to observe a portion of the spirited University of Texas Longhorns football game from a distance. Later, we rode around the area near all of the food trucks and tailgate parties, with an area full of excited fans dressed in their Longhorn gear of burnt orange and white. On the front page of the Sunday newspaper the following day, I saw the score of the football game: UT won against Kansas, 35-13. Go Longhorns!

We continued our pleasant Saturday afternoon sightseeing excursion as Aundria drove by the Capital building. She parked the car, and the three of us leisurely walked around the meticulously manicured grounds, where we saw even more beautiful scenes of Autumn on the picture-perfect October day. We leisurely walked near the surrounding trees and shrubbery. "What a gorgeous fall Saturday afternoon in Austin," I said to my mother and goddaughter. They nodded in total agreement as the three of us continued to slowly stroll along the walkways while crunching the clusters of dry leaves that we stepped on when we wandered through the pathways.

The next day, we watched a church service on television, and afterward, I decided to spend the remainder of the Sabbath Day resting and reading. My mother and her granddaughter watched movies while sharing snacks and catching up on their past lives. Everyone was happy.

After a day indoors, we had the urge to get out, stretch our legs, and walk in the sunshine. We were ready for more sightseeing. Mom let us know that she wanted a new pocketbook, referring to a purse, so Aundria took us to the shopping mall and there my mother found an attractive handbag. The pocketbook she selected was a perfect color of pink for a mature lady, a soft shade of raspberry. She really liked her new pocketbook, especially when Aundrea told her how good she looked with it. Mom proudly held the handles of the bag near her waist and strutted a few lively steps as she modeled her new pocketbook clutched by her side while smiling and strutting back and forth in front of us. Yes, indeed, "that's my Mamma," I proudly proclaimed.

We had an enjoyable time with my goddaughter and my mother's newest granddaughter. She and her Grandma Grace, as she affectionately refers to Mamma, are incredibly fond of each other. To show appreciation for her hospitality, I wanted to leave a parting gift and decided to bake a couple of sweet potato pies. Aundria and I share many loves and food is definitely one of them. She prepared a Mexican feast of carne asada, chicken enchiladas and Pico de Gallo with rice and beans for dinner, our last supper in Austin. The three of us ended our visit with great memories of Austin, Texas.

12: Everyone Forgets Sometimes!

Time passed, and Mamma and I were adjusting well to our new living arrangements. She started to follow a healthy routine while taking her daily medications and vitamins and eating wholesome and nutritious meals. We took daily walks in the neighborhood park and joined a water aerobics class at the nearby gym. Physically, she appeared stronger, and I thought my mother was probably in the best physical condition that she could be. She was adapting to her new lifestyle.

When I scheduled an appointment for her physical examination, I thought all was well. Unfortunately, her medical report was not what I expected. The doctor diagnosed her with early-onset Alzheimer's Disease, which was a heavy blow. I was not prepared for such drastic news and asked God how to handle this. I prayed for guidance, and He told me to be still and wait on Him. The results were difficult to receive, and I did not share the information with my mother.

For the test to determine Alzheimer's, the doctor asked Mamma to draw a clock with the time of 10:00 displayed on it. She did not successfully complete the task in the required time limit. She could tell time, but she could **not** draw a clock. The next question she was asked was, "What city do you live in?" Mamma had recently moved to Denver and did not give the right answer. I was so proud of her for the one correct response she gave when she stated the name of the then-current President of the United States, Barack Obama! Then she proudly added, "And his pretty wife is, "Michelle Obama!"

Although my mother had hardly any formal education when she was younger, she is definitely a quick learner. I realized that when I taught her to read, several years ago. Sometimes, when we are sitting close together, I can hear her reading aloud, and occasionally, she breaks words into syllables, a method she learned to help her pronounce words from "our reading lessons." I am so proud of my mother. She is a champion life learner! Yes, Mamma forgets things occasionally and she is always quick to remind me, "Baby, everyone forgets something sometimes, even you. She is absolutely correct! My mother continues to have a good quality of life as she manages to keep a positive outlook.

She encourages me and frequently tells me, "Baby, it's going to be alright!" Even when I do not see a positive outcome, I know it will eventually occur. That is called **having faith** and my level of faith has increased tremendously, thanks to God and Miss Grace.

There are days when I remind myself of all of our **many** advantages. Mamma adjusts well to changes, she is physically strong, and the bonus blessing is that she continues to enjoy traveling and does it well. The lady is not a "wanderer" and that is another blessing. Because we travel so frequently, I ordered the Medic Alert necklace as a security device in case of an emergency.

Miss Grace is not shy at all, and she definitely lets me know what she wants and when she wants it. I remember an occasion when we had to rush to board our plane on time. As soon as we were seated, she immediately told me she was hungry and wanted a meal. The attendant who was standing in first class overheard our conversation from our front-row seats in coach when I read the list of sandwiches from the menu.

Before she could select an item, he offered her a jumbo shrimp cocktail, which she readily accepted. He politely informed me that only one was available and it was specifically for her! While I munched on a dry turkey and cheese sandwich with wilted lettuce, Mamma enjoyed her meal. She sort of flaunted it a bit as she smiled at me while she devoured bites of the delicious-looking dish. As she finished her meal, she glanced at me and asked, "Oh, did you want one?" She grinned and I just smiled. I thanked God that she has maintained her delightful sense of humor!

Another thing about Miss Grace is that she is a people magnet and has such a pleasant disposition. God has given her these gifts, and she has maintained them throughout her years. When we are out and about, Mamma likes to sit on the park bench, relax, and enjoy the warmth of the sunshine.

Frequently, a person will sit next to her and start a friendly conversation. A few minutes later, my mother and her new acquaintance are chatting like long, lost buddies. There are times when we are shopping, and I leave the area for a few minutes only to return and observe another customer asking her which items match or what outfit looks best. A fellow shopper solicits Mom's advice, and she frankly offers it like a top fashion expert. This happens frequently and it always ends with a complete stranger acting like her "best buddy!" It must be her charming personality and cute little smile!

12: Renewed And Restored

With all of the recent changes in our lives, we definitely needed support to adjust to the numerous transformations. Since I did not know where to begin, I sought the Lord, and he answered. When I contacted the Alzheimer's Association, doors opened for us. They recommended an Adult Day Center, and we scheduled an appointment for the next day.

My mother had lunch with the participants, and she made friends the same day. The Director gave me a complete tour of the modern and well-equipped facility and explained the extensive programs. The curriculum was impressive. It included a wide variety of sessions such as history lessons, current news, music and dancing, field trips, daily exercises, and walks in the enclosed garden. The activities and the staff were remarkable! I was pleased to enroll Mamma in such an extraordinary program for adults with Alzheimer's.

During the tour of the facility, the remarkable director greeted all of the clients and employees by their names, and I noticed they were not wearing name tags. My mother and I agreed that this was definitely the right place for her. We enrolled her that day, and she attended sessions the following week and enjoyed herself.

It was amazing that at her age she was learning so much and experiencing a completely new life. Mamma enjoyed attending the Center, especially on the days they had dancing and music with a live musician. Miss Grace quickly advanced in that class and became "Queen" of the dance floor.

On the other hand, living in the large metropolitan city of Denver, Colorado, was a major adjustment for her. Her current residence and surroundings were so different from her previous home in rural Alabama. She did not like where we lived at all! It was a high-rise building near the downtown area, and most of the time, my mother pushed the wrong elevator button and got lost in "that big ole building!"

When I sought solutions to our problems, we found them. After a few changes and some minor adjustments, our problems were resolved. I waited in the lobby for Mamma to arrive and we took the elevator together. She even allowed me the privilege to push the elevator button for her, and later, she automatically did it on her own. Change can be difficult, especially for the elderly, but we must always remember that we are never alone. God is the greatest changemaker. With prayer and patience, our situations did improve.

Shortly afterward, another door opened, and this one was for me. Our church offered a Diabetes Self-Management Class, and I enrolled and attended the sessions. The program was beneficial since I had been diagnosed with diabetes. The bonus blessing occurred at the end of the course when the facilitator for the class asked me to become an instructor. Thanks to the Ameri-Corps for Seniors Program, I received detailed training and preparation, and soon became an employee with the Center for African American Health. Mamma was in an excellent program on one side of town, and I was participating in a remarkable project at the other end of Denver. With a bit of time and coordination, we operated on a schedule that worked well for both of us.

13: Grace's Flower Garden

For years, my mother had one of the prettiest flower gardens that bloomed in the yard surrounding her home in Alabama. With the warm southern temperatures, the plants grew year-round. Every spring the bright colored tulips and daffodils announced the opening of the season. Prime spots were reserved for her prized and hardy rose bushes, which she pruned and nourished to grow into such stately and elegant beauties. The sweetest flowers, the robust honeysuckle bushes, grew in clusters and they flourished on the sunny side of the house, near the kitchen windows. By the peak of spring, all of the red, pink, and white azaleas filled her garden. Occasionally, their beautiful blooms lasted well into the autumn of the year. Sometimes several of her beautiful flowers maintained large, robust blossoms during the fall and winter months when the warmer temperatures continued.

All of those attractive varieties of flowers gave my mother pride and satisfaction. She missed working in the yard which was so rewarding and therapeutic for her. Unfortunately, that pleasure disappeared when she moved to Denver. Of course, I knew the issue involved more than her garden. The transition was difficult and the relocation to my home was a major change. Most of all, Mamma missed her former life that included so many of her family members, lifelong friends, church congregation and neighbors in her former hometown. Yes, she yearned for the return of her familiar life and the lady was a bit sad in spite of my efforts to offer cheerful and entertaining activities for her.

When winter arrived in Denver, my mother sat near the window looking sort of sad and a bit forlorn at the barren park across the street. There was not a flower in sight nor a blade of green grass to be seen. The floral bouquets that I gave her produced a slight smile and a little "thank you" but she really missed all that she had left behind. The comfort of the familiar had disappeared from her life and it was not easy for her to embrace her new environment.

At the Center for Seniors, where Mamma had recently enrolled, she participated in the **Making Memories Program**. Now, she was taking art classes with an instructor who taught drawing and painting lessons for elderly adults living with early Alzheimer's. I was pleased that my mother was willing to learn something new at this stage in her life, especially since she usually does not like to try different things.

The program helped her to discover a way to recapture portions of the pride and enjoyment from the flower garden in Alabama through her paintings. God had given Mamma new tools to work with; a canvas, a few brushes, and an array of colorful paints. She learned a different way to discover another source of enjoyment and gratification when she used different techniques to create beautiful images of the brightly colored blossoms that grew in the yard of her home in Alabama. Her artworks began to adorn the walls of our home. As time passed, my mother continued her art lessons and her newly discovered talent gave her a wonderful sense of pride and accomplishment.

Our family was so proud of her! We never knew that she could draw a stick figure, but now, the lady is creating drawings and paintings that are beautiful works of art. As her interest grows, she improves. Mamma won an award as "Artist of the Month" for her painting of beautiful flowers. Her award-winning work was featured in a gallery.

14: Dealing With The Loneliness

The Alzheimer's Association held a symposium, and the main speakers for the seminar were a select group consisting of a physician, a psychologist, and a therapist. Afterward, a small group of caregivers participated on a panel. Since I had previously attended sessions with support groups, I was asked to participate with the group and briefly describe my caregiving experiences. I thought I would not have much to discuss because my mother is more like a companion than a patient and she does not require extensive care.

While listening to the other caregivers' responses, I was surprised when a lady from the audience asked me a question specifically. She asked, "How do you deal with loneliness?"

Immediately I replied, "This is a powerful question!" Slowly, I took a few deep breaths and tried to process her question. "This is going to be tough," I thought to myself as tears immediately came to my eyes before I could respond. Not only was this a complicated question, but it was also something I never thought about! As I wondered how to respond, my tears started flowing. "Well," I sighed, "I will try to answer the question as soon as I wipe some of these tears away." Someone from the audience handed me a box of tissues.

When I recovered as best as I could, I replied, "One way I try to handle the situation is by doing what I am doing now, learning more about Alzheimer's. My feelings often fluctuate up and down as I try to keep a handle on my emotions. At my first counseling session, I was told to journal. Writing helps me to freely express my thoughts. I can write about our experiences better than I can verbally express them. Also, it seems that writing my feelings on paper is a way to observe our situation from a different perspective. Writing helps to capture memories of my mother as well as record the new experiences that we are currently creating. The memories we make today will enrich our lives tomorrow. Also, I hope our journey will help others in some way."

That was my response to a question years ago at a conference, and today, I am really glad that I recorded so many of our experiences. Frequently, I have thought about the lady's question, "How do you handle the loneliness?" I have extended my answer, "Sometimes, I cry and that is good!" Time has taught me that it is good to cry sometimes. Tears can be a way to wash our eyes and clear our vision. Weeping is not always sorrowful; it can also be therapeutic. I do not believe we should tell a person **not** to cry, because there are times when we **need** to cry because a 'good' cry can make us feel so much better. Sometimes tears can soften our hearts to make us more agreeable to change. Also, I think of tears as "one of "God's mechanisms" to cleanse and strengthen us!"

A friend once described tears **as *liquid prayers***. She continued to tell me that she believes God saves our tears and He collects them so that our tears can be returned to us! Could it be? God recycles our tears and returns them as blessings! Our tears may account for the blessings that we receive during our lifetimes, too numerous to count! Sometimes, I cry, and I always feel so much better afterward as God gives me the strength to move forward. I believe my mother has lived as well and as long as she has because of all the unconditional love that she has received, all of the Grace that God has given Grace!

Throughout the years, I have learned that "time heals all of our wounds when we do not continue to peel the scalps off and rehearse our pains." Ironically, time takes time, but only when we allow it to do its work will we become healed. Yes, we will be restored and completely renewed in time!

15: Mammograms – Two In One Day

With all of the changes that my mother and I experienced last year, time passed so quickly! When January arrived, it occurred to me that we had not taken our annual breast examinations. In order to save time, I scheduled both of the appointments on the same day. When the day arrived, I said to myself, regretfully, "What were you thinking? Why did you schedule both of the exams on the same day? That was a **big** mistake!"

This was an extremely difficult situation and too much to handle. I realized I should have allowed more time between the appointments to address my mother's apprehensions and her concerns. Constantly I had to reassure her that she did not have breast cancer simply because she was getting an examination of her breasts. In the midst of all of the frustrations, I prayed and yes, God answered. The receptionist noticed that we were having a difficult time, and she offered to help me complete the paperwork.

Afterward, she initiated a friendly conversation with my mother. The young lady told Mamma her name was Rebecca, which is my mother's middle name. Then she turned toward me and softly whispered that her mother had dementia. Rebecca

Traveling Down the Road With Grace

was extraordinary! Her kind and gentle manner helped my mother to relax, and she calmed me down as well.

When we entered the examination room, there was a framed poster on the wall, **"CARE IS AN ACT OF GRACE!"** I smiled as I looked upward and said, "Thank you, Lord!" My mother's examination was extensive and required additional time. Mamma told me repeatedly that she did not want to be "bothered with any of this mess," as she referred to having the mammogram. "She will be alright," I constantly reminded myself. Yes, by having a kind technician to assist us, Mamma did great! Afterward, Rebecca was at the door when my mother's X-rays were completed, and she led her to the dressing room; then, she held the door open for me to enter the examination room for my turn. The young receptionist smiled and told me that she would stay with my mother and keep her occupied. I felt as though God had sent me a "new best friend." We successfully made it through the two mammograms that day. When we finished, I realized the experience was not that challenging, after all. I thanked God for sending us an angel. Yes, God is so good! He had us a wonderful angel named Rebecca!

16: The Coldest Day In January

It is a bitter cold day, and the sun is shining so brightly but I cannot feel a bit of its warmth. All that I feel is the freezing chill through my heavy wool coat and I am very cold! It was an extremely long walk through the hospital's parking lot to the doctor's office for the return visit to discuss my mother's recent mammogram. When I finally arrived at the office, I hastily accepted the steaming cup of hot coffee that the receptionist offered me before meeting with my mother's physician.

The Oncologist thoroughly explained the details of my mother's X-rays, which revealed a positive result. Although she officially told me the results today, God revealed the message to me yesterday in the dressing room. I saw those adorable little teddy bears and read the brochure explaining their history and the information about the creators of the cute little bears. Afterward, I gently picked up one that was on display and cradled the lovable stuffed figure that had HOPE inscribed all over its small body in my arms.

When I tenderly held the adorable stuffed animal, the revelation came to me: "Mom will get one of these!" Yes, my mother would receive a Hope Bear, and I knew what owning one meant. Tears started to roll down my cheeks. God had spoken, and I had heard Him! I dried my eyes and turned around just in time to see Mamma walking toward me. She smiled and said, "Baby, I'm alright!"

    I tried as hard as I could to pretend that I was, too. This is a hard pill to swallow! Alzheimer's can be difficult, and cancer can become problematic. Neither is preferable to the other since they both can be dreadful. What does a person do when their mother has been diagnosed with both? Well, I just found out and I do not know what to do! I must wait to hear from God! When the oncologist discussed a treatment for my mother, the first question I asked was, "What effect would the cancer treatment have on Alzheimer's disease?" Her physician explained that there was no information available. She told me that the research for the medicine had not been done on a patient diagnosed with Alzheimer's. I was explicitly instructed to always ask physicians and pharmacists about the effects of any medication on a person with Alzheimer's before it was given to her. Therefore, after much prayer and additional consultation, I made the final decision for my mother not to receive the doctor's recommended treatment. My response was no to the medication, but **YES** to the following:

Daily Communion-Faith and Hope in God Anointing with Blessed Oil-Reading Healing Scriptures-Frequent and Fervent Prayer

This was a difficult decision to make, and I did not resolve it lightly. After lots of prayer and all of the factors considered, I was comfortable with my decision. Mamma had been through so much during the recent years of her life and had many traumatic experiences. My mother's husband, for more than thirty years, died of cancer. Her best friend of seventy years also died of cancer. The total number of our immediate family members and friends who died of cancer is more than I can count. I am at peace with my decision. I prayed and God answered!

We did take the HOPE Bear home, and she sits on the dresser as a daily reminder of the HOPE that God has given us. Mamma never asked me about the Bear, nor did I discuss it with her. It was just too difficult to say out loud. Although I could not talk about it, I could write about it, and I could pray about it. We both believe, "By his stripes we were healed!"

My mother received the cancer diagnosis when she was eighty-three years old. I thank God there are cancer survivors in their nineties and now the world has another one, Grace Rebecca! Like my Mamma always says, "Baby, what's gonna' be is gonna' be!"

17: **Purple for Royalty & Alzheimer's**

Time and time again, my mother has been a true warrior. The lady never ceases to amaze me, and I admire her strong spirit. One morning she woke up with inflamed and puffy eyes. The following day her cheeks were swollen and enlarged. She looked as though she had been in a boxing match and lost the last few rounds. Fortunately, I was able to schedule an appointment with her physician that afternoon and she was diagnosed with a severe sinus infection.

Mamma took the prescribed medication for her ailment, and the situation started to improve, but the inflammation left shedding, dry skin on her entire face, which did not look attractive at all! After going through all of that and seeing her face, she did not want to cancel our next planned trip, and we were scheduled to travel in a few days. Her face looked terrible but since she wanted to go, we continued our plans. Mamma told me, "Baby, I'll be alright! It will get better, and besides, I can wear a pair of those sunglasses!"

Would you believe, she had been given a pair of beautiful new sunglasses from the Alzheimer's Association Conference that we attended the week before her facial condition occurred? The sunglasses actually covered a portion of the distorted skin and as Mamma says, "He always sends us what we need, when we need it."

The lady put on her beautiful new purple sunglasses and stylishly draped a fashionable purple shawl around her shoulders as she strutted through the airport looking absolutely fabulous! Yes indeed, Queen Grace was back in the air, flying high and looking fabulous as we continued our plans to travel. We arrived at our destination, Gary, Indiana, our previous hometown for many years. We visited relatives and long-term friends and had a wonderful time. After all, there is no place like home.

18: May I Present, Queen Grace!

It is so easy to recognize my mother's regal qualities: her royal pose when she is stylishly dressed and ready to make an entrance, the tilt of her head, and the way she places her church hat on her head as though she wears a crown. Her style exhibits royalty when she is exquisitely donned from head to toe, and her cute, sly smile reflects wisdom.

As her daughter and caregiver, I know her story. I am totally aware of the regeneration that occurred in my mother's life during the last few years. God completely renewed her physically and mentally and made her stronger than before! The Master restored and returned her strength, beauty, and peace. Mamma was crowned queen, not just for a day but for the remainder of her life. In one day, her life's journey elevated her to the level of royalty.

MISS GRACE WAS DESIGNATED QUEEN!

For her coronation, she was dressed in a lovely royal blue dress and adorned with a crown. She was presented with a dozen beautiful long-stemmed red roses and had a smile on her face so bright it could light the darkness!

My mother was crowned Queen of the Senior Prom! This particular coronation was by no means ordinary, it was extraordinary! First of all, the lady is nearly ninety years old, and she attends an Adult Day Center. Secondly, she never graduated from high school, not to mention previously attended a prom! Thirdly, her escort for this auspicious event is her favorite grandson, who had flown on a "red eye" flight for the day to serve as her escort for such an extraordinary occasion. Also, her coronation and her grandson's arrival were both complete surprises for her. The lady's face lit up like a bright sun when the announcement was made, and her name was called. Her handsome escort proudly strutted into the ballroom and gently secured her hand as he guided the Queen to her throne.

It was hard to determine who enjoyed the Senior Prom the most, Queen Grace or Grandson Reginald. They stayed on the dance floor while entertaining their audience. This event was the first time the two of them had danced together, and they realized it was an activity they thoroughly enjoyed. Their moves and steps were so synchronized that one would have thought they had practiced for hours, as they appeared to be having the time of their lives.

After the ball was over, the crown was placed on a closet shelf with the purple sash neatly folded under it and the roses eventually faded. Except for the many pictures and a video, that day has become a memory, but the reality of the Queen's royal status still remains. The event occurred years ago but the result still lingers. Occasionally, I observe my mother from a distance, and I see a slight lift of her head and a soft, shrewd smile so unassumingly spreads across her face as she pauses to pose in front of the mirror before she exits the room. I smile, too, as I say to myself, "Go On, Queen Grace!"

Once again, God has taught us, no matter how old you are, how far down you have been, regardless of the tragedy that has stricken you, He can always lift you up! When He lifts you, He takes you higher than you ever thought you could go. We can never give up on God. Surely, He has not given up on us.

Traveling Down the Road With Grace

19: Laughter And Love

    These days, my mother and I are experiencing the best years of our lives together. Occasionally, we may have a tad of friction for a moment or two, but we manage to live together with lots of peace and good times. Naturally, we have similar perspectives on most issues, after all, we were cut from the same fabric. There are times when we complete each other's sentences and usually, one knows what the other wants before the request is made. Mom and I are strongly connected, and I am grateful to continuously learn sage wisdom from her. Just the other day, Mamma gave me a lesson on the importance of laughter and love in our daily lives and she made it 'as clear as a bell.'

    I had the bright idea to clean the refrigerator, which was in desperate need of some warm water, soap, and lots of elbow grease. I began the dreadful chore by removing all of the items from the refrigerator, and afterward, I very carefully detached the shelves, compartments, and removable parts, which I thoroughly washed and dried. Then I thought, "That was easy, no problem."

    I was satisfied and started to feel good about the job and proudly proclaimed, "If I knew it was going to be this easy, I would have done it a long time ago!" The chore was a little time-consuming but not complicated at all. I easily completed the task of placing all the pieces back, by simply sliding the moveable parts into place, or so I thought. Finally, I closed the refrigerator door and wiped it sparkling clean, only to discover there was an extra part still remaining on the kitchen counter. "Oh, no," I thought with a bit of frustration. I tried desperately to fit the lone part into the right spot, all to no avail when I finally realized I could not put a round peg into a square hole.

    My mother must have heard my fidgeting and grumbling because she came and stood in the kitchen doorway. When she saw what I was trying to do, she pulled up a chair and without saying a word, sat in full view of the refrigerator and me. Having her as an audience added more to my frustration and immediately, I suggested, "Mamma, why don't you go in your room and watch television?" She immediately responded, "Oh, no! I'll just sit here for a while," as she let out a little muffled laughter.

    I continued to fidget with the odd part as I tried to connect the tiny piece of hardware to the spot where it belonged. Soon, a big smile spread across her face, and she started giggling and her laughter increased. I caught a portion of her cheerful spirit, and we were both laughing! My mother's humor was the therapy that I needed. Her laughter was music to my ears, and it reminded me that the situation was not serious at all. As our contagious laughter continued to increase, I realized that I had not heard my mother laugh in a long time. Then it occurred to me that I had not laughed recently either. It felt **so** good to be laughing, and suddenly, we both were giggling like little girls!

I walked close to Mamma, threw my arms around her, and gave her lots of *big, sloppy kisses* on her cheeks! She responded, "Girl, **gone** away from here!" I continued to fill her forehead and cheeks with my sporadic kisses because I knew she was enjoying the large doses of love and affection and we both liked all of the fun and laughter. I started dancing around her and singing repeatedly:

"I love you a bushel and a peck
and a hug around the neck."

Gradually, I finished my little dramatic performance, but before I did, I wondered if she remembered the times when she sang that little ditty to me when I was a little girl and I giggled when she sang and danced with me. I did not ask her because I really wanted to linger in the loving memories that we just shared. Love always feels so good! If laughter is medicine for the soul, and I believe it is, my mother's laughter gave me an enormous dose.

Alright, now what about that missing part from the refrigerator that was left on the kitchen counter? What happened to it? I am so glad you asked! Let me tell you. The next day, I repeated the task after I asked Mamma if she would help me with the chore, and she agreed to join me. Again, I removed all of the items from the refrigerator, and as we were placing the shelves back in place, Mamma put "the missing part" in her hand, spotted the corner where it belonged, and easily slid it into place. The spot was hardly visible, in the back on the bottom shelf.

She did not say a word when she turned and smiled at me and I thought to myself, "That's my Mamma! I really love her," and I told her so as I repeatedly planted a few more kisses on her cheeks. When the job was finally completed, we celebrated with dishes of ice cream, a high five and a few more smiles. I thought to myself "It is amazing what a person can learn from a little old lady with Alzheimer's!"

20: New England In The Fall

Several decades ago, my mother lived in New Haven, Connecticut. When her grandson was a little fellow, we visited her for Christmas and flew on United Airlines for our first airplane ride. That was more than fifty years ago, and I still remember our beautiful and serene snow filled Christmas holiday in Connecticut that we shared with Mamma so long ago. When I learned about a trip to New England, I knew I wanted to return to the area, and I thought Mamma would enjoy the excursion also.

The tour included traveling to several New England states in the fall of the year, which seemed like a fantastic trip, and it would also offer a different type of traveling experience for us. We would be with a large group of people as opposed to just the two of us. This would be an excellent opportunity for both of us to interact with other travelers. When I discussed some of the details of group travel, she was agreeable. After all, my mother is a natural "people magnet." She mixes well and I do not believe she has ever met a stranger in her entire life. I thought it might be interesting for us to try something different and joining a tour was our way to sort of "spread our wings."

We started the arrangements for our next mother-daughter trip and prepared for our upcoming journey. My mother is a nature lover, and the tour is in the fall of the year when Mother Nature does some of her most exquisite work and the scenery should be spectacular. Having the heart of an educator, I expect to discover many "hidden" lessons, and I was also prepared to learn more new information and highlights about our great country, such as the following:

Early American history books record the story of Captain John Smith who sailed to Massachusetts Bay in 1614 and befriended the Indian tribe living there.

Afterward, he distributed a map of the area and named it New England, which was appealing to the English people who crossed the ocean and settled in the new land. More than 150 years later, the American Revolution occurred on the soil of the city that became Boston, Massachusetts.

The city is steeped in American history and has a diverse population. It is the only state capital in the contiguous United States with an oceanic coastline.

Traveling Down the Road With Grace

    We arrived in Boston the day before the tour began in order to explore a bit on our own. On our first day in Boston, we walked to the Quincy Market and wandered about, exploring the North End, and realized we had entered a Foodie's Paradise. When we discovered the area of several restaurants and markets, we agreed it was a great time to have lunch, which consisted of the freshest, best-tasting seafood, and our meal was delicious.

    Afterwards, we leisurely strolled through the Boston Commons, among the street musicians and entertainers. The weather was ideal, and we appreciated the refreshing breezes gently blowing across the Atlantic Ocean. We enjoyed the scenery and the pleasant climate as we walked together, arm-in-arm, among the sparse crowd. I thought to myself, "what a significant time to enjoy this period of our lives! What a blessing, a mother and daughter, both in the autumn of their lives, walking together while enjoying the autumn of the year!

    Later that evening we dressed to celebrate our first evening in Boston and we dined at the hotel's restaurant. The waiter seated us at a table near a large window which was filled with the stunning nighttime views of the Boston Harbor that appeared in the background. While we were enjoying the classical music, I noticed Mamma was smiling and occasionally glancing out the window. "Uh huh!" I softly muttered under my breath and smiled back at her. It was so obvious, she was enjoying the beautiful and serene surroundings, the relaxing music and having a wonderful time. "I knew she would," I thought to myself. As a matter of fact, we were both enjoying ourselves and this is just the beginning!

During times like these, I feel God's strong and restorative power surrounding us. I can see the joy in my mother's eyes, and I am so pleased. What God has given us we must cherish and appreciate every day. I shudder to think what our lives would be like if we had not chosen to make changes and live together. Thank God we both can enjoy this wonderful period in our lives jointly. God has given us more than I ever thought or imagined, and I am so grateful.

21: The Official Tour Begins

The following day, we boarded the tour bus and our travel guide, a native Bostonian, greeted a completely full bus of travelers. He welcomed the group and officially announced the beginning of our expedition.

Our first stop was at the Faneuil Hall, the Cradle of Liberty, in Boston, Massachusetts, the capital of the state. It is one of the oldest cities in the United States as well as the largest city in New England. It was at Boston's Old North Church, where Paul Revere began his legendary ride and also where we heard a docent deliver the famous poem written by Henry Wadsworth Longfellow.

PAUL REVERE'S MIDNIGHT RIDE

Listen, my children, and you shall hear
Of the midnight ride of Paul Revere,
On the eighteenth of April, in Seventy-five.
Hardly a man is now alive who
remembers that famous day and
year. He said to his friend,
"If the British march by land or sea
from the town tonight,
Hang a lantern aloft in the belfry arch Of the
North Church tower as a signal light
One, if by land, and two, if by sea;
And I on the opposite shore will be,
Ready to ride and spread the alarm
Through every Middlesex village and farm, for
the country folk to be up and to arm."

Traveling Down the Road With Grace

    That afternoon, we passed the State Capital and the Boston Commons as we continued our ride to Lexington, Massachusetts, where the Minutemen had their first Revolutionary skirmish. Our tour continued to the Lexington Battle Green, where we followed Paul Revere's route from Lexington to Concord. This was the site where the "shot heard around the world" on April 19, 1775, signaled the start of the American Revolutionary War.

    We stopped and viewed the Old North Bridge from a distance. It was not opened because the Government of the United States was closed! The federal administration was shut down from October 1 to 16, 2013, because our political parties could not agree on a budget. The tour continued as we traveled through rural New England and passed several old stonewalls that reminded me of lines from Robert Frost's poem.

Mending Walls

Something there is that doesn't love a wall,
That sends the frozen groundswell under it
And spills the upper boulders in the sun.

Most of these walls have an "abandoned" look with a few gaps between them. The stonewalls were placed years ago, and they seemed to blend naturally into the New England landscape. We learned that Massachusetts is a true "stonewall country." Most of the stonewalls in the region were built during the century of 1750–1850. These walls were constructed by using the simple principle of just laying the rocks one on top of the other.

This is called the "Dry Wall" approach and provides for excellent drainage, which is why the walls have survived to this day. At one time, it was estimated that there were more than 250,000 miles of stonewalls in the northeast, with most of them in the New England region, and about half of these still remain to this day.

While we were traveling through the streets of Concord, Massachusetts, it was a delight to see the home of Louisa May Alcott, a favorite childhood author of many young readers. Just imagine her sitting near an upstairs window as she penned her famous book, <u>Little Women</u>, which tells the story of

Traveling Down the Road With Grace

the lives of her sisters, from childhood to womanhood. We travelled a bit further and viewed the home of Nathaniel Hawthorne.

Seeing his residence reminded me of the time in my high school English literature class when we read his novel, <u>The Scarlet Letter.</u> He wrote the story of the indelible "A" of Hester Prynne, a teenage girl, about my age at that time. Afterwards, we saw the home of Ralph Waldo Emerson and the woods where Thoreau's cabin once stood on Walden's Pond. Traveling through those areas was like wandering into a live version of an Early American literature book with a bit of vivid imagination, of course.

Our New England tour headed south, and we stopped at the most famous rock in America, Plymouth Rock, where pilgrims from the Mayflower landed in 1620. Next, the group traveled to Cape Cod's southern shore for a stay at a resort in the popular and affluent community of Hyannis Port, the site of President John F. Kennedy's summer White House. It is located in the residential town of Barnstable, Massachusetts. This region is also the location of the John F. Kennedy Hyannis Museum, the John F. Kennedy Memorial, and the Massachusetts Air and Space Museum.

Traveling Down the Road With Grace

A Pictorial of Traveling with Grace!

Traveling Down the Road With Grace

Queen Grace

Traveling Down the Road With Grace

Mom (Grace) and Daddy (Willie Joe):

Joann as a young Girl

Traveling Down the Road With Grace

Grace all over the Place

Traveling Down the Road With Grace

Grace, Enjoying Everything

Joann Marrying Mr. Bobby Wilson.

Traveling Down the Road With Grace

Visit to Detroit: At MOTOWN

Grace Being Grace

Traveling Down the Road With Grace

Traveling with Miss Grace

Traveling Down the Road With Grace

Miss Grace and Joann

Traveling Down the Road With Grace

The GREAT Miss Grace

Traveling Down the Road With Grace

Our last train ride!

Grace Living her life

Traveling Down the Road With Grace

Always Together

Traveling Down the Road With Grace

Grace Seeing the Sights

Traveling Down the Road With Grace

Grace with Joann and her Grandaughters

Traveling Down the Road With Grace

Grace, Joann, and Granddaughter

Traveling Down the Road With Grace

Mackenzies Illustrations

Acknowledgments

I am profoundly grateful to my granddaughter, Mackenzie Grace, whose artistic talent and deep love for **Great Grace** and me illuminates the pages of this book.

Her illustrations not only bring our stories to life but also capture the essence of our shared journey.

Thank you, Mackenzie, for your dedication and for infusing this work with your heartfelt creativity.

Traveling Down the Road With Grace

Grace with Joann

Traveling Down the Road With Grace

Grace the Prom Queen

Traveling Down the Road With Grace

Alright, Now, the Lady Can Dance

22: The Splendor Of New England

We boarded a ferry from Woods Hole to Martha's Vineyard, the town named for a European sailor's daughter, Martha, who became famous because she found wild grapes growing on the island. This summer colony is very peaceful and serene, making it appealing as a refuge for various individuals.

This unique community is naturally designed to serve as a sanctuary, and its early inhabitants arrived seeking freedom within the abolition movement in the year 1787. Perhaps that is why a preacher and former slave selected this location for that specific purpose. When Rev. John Saunders arrived at this region, he encouraged people in the community to unite and assist previously oppressed people of color and help them obtain their freedom and the Vineyard became a renowned getaway for Black families since the 1800s.

As time passed, this land's beauty and peaceful atmosphere offered an abundance of inspiration and creativity for professionals and celebrities who pursued the comfortable and relaxing lifestyle of the island. The Vineyard is a natural attraction for professional artists and writers. This remarkably charming community is located off the coast of

Massachusetts and can only be reached by either airplane or boat.

After a brief ride on a ferry, our group of tourists spent the day wandering among the unique "gingerbread cottages" throughout the town. The homes resemble an enchanted fairytale land with a few hundred beautiful, brightly colored dwellings adorned with dainty trimmings. The attractive residences have unique names such as "Angel Cottage," "Wooden Valentine," and "Pink House."

My mother and I leisurely wandered around this scenic area, occasionally stopping to enjoy the beautiful scenery. We especially enjoyed the fresh ocean breezes as we walked among the huge oak trees. Occasionally, we stopped to admire the beautiful blooming flowers, and Mamma identified a few of the blossoms that grew along the trails where we walked. When the day ended, we joined our group of fellow tourists and returned to Cape Cod.

The next segment of the tour was in Newport, Rhode Island, the world's sailing capital. There, we toured the historic Vanderbilt "summer cottage," The Breakers, which covers thirteen acres of land. This Italian Renaissance-style palace has seventy rooms and is the absolute grandest of all the Newport estates. It is often referred to as the "Gilded Age" mansion and was built in the 1890s as a summer home for the "extremely well-to-do" Vanderbilt family. It is probably the most luxurious summer mansion in the region, with its spectacular views of the eastern Atlantic coastline.

23: The Magnificent Mountains!

The next morning, the tour got underway with a drive on the scenic road leading to Plymouth Notch, the birthplace of President Calvin Coolidge. Our 30th President took the oath of office in a ceremony presided over by his father beside the light of a kerosene lamp in the parlor of his family home. I told my mother that she and the President's wife share the same first name, Grace, and she responded with her usual look.

Many reminders of a bygone era surrounded the former President's home. Seeing all of the antique artifacts reminded me of the past, and immediately, I wandered among the memorabilia that surrounded the large farm and the beautiful countryside. I was so busy admiring the antique artifacts and taking pictures that it took me a while to realize my mother was not nearby. "Where could she be?" I wondered and immediately turned around and walked back on the pathway leading to the president's residence. Soon, I spotted Mamma from a distance. She was sitting in a rocking chair on the front porch of the former President's home. The lady had comfortably placed herself there, rocking back and forth, as though she was sitting on her very own porch, and this was where she belonged!

Traveling Down the Road With Grace

    From a distance, I could clearly see her and the other tourists who casually passed by her. They smiled and cordially spoke, and she pleasantly returned their greetings. I grinned as I shook my head and said, "That's my Mamma!" Together, we left President Coolidge's front porch and headed to our tour bus to join our fellow travelers.

    On this beautiful autumn day, we were riding along the roads of the New England countryside while passing through the charming villages, which were filled with tall, white steeples that adorned the tops of the multiple churches located in the area. Suddenly, the bus turned into a parking lot next to a gigantic statue and stopped. We learned that we were parked next to the Bennington Battle Monument. Out in the middle of what appeared to be nowhere stood an enormous 306-foot and four and ½ inches tall stone obelisk, which was completed and dedicated in 1891.

    This structure was built to commemorate the Battle of Bennington, which occurred on August 16, 1777, and is considered to be the actual turning point for the Revolutionary War. Perhaps the purpose of coming to this location was to view another historical memorial, but it also offered us bird' s-eye views of the fantastic foliage as far away as we could see. At the Battle Monument, we could observe the landscape and the surrounding region for miles and miles.

Traveling Down the Road With Grace

It was great for people like Mom and me since we did not have to climb multiple steps to reach the top. We simply stepped into the modern-day elevator, pushed the button, and rode all the way to the top of the tall structure in order to see even more fantastic views from a much further distance. The area was beautiful as far as we could see! I whispered a little "Thank You!" to Mr. Elisha Otis, the imaginative craftsman who produced the first passenger elevator. Mamma and I, along with other sightseers, proceeded to reach such unbelievable heights to observe these stunning views.

Later, we enter the magnificent White Mountains that serve as a striking backdrop for the stunning autumn foliage that appears to stretch all the way across Lake Winnipesaukee. The colors of the various leaves on the trees are magnificent! They are brilliantly bright yellow, vibrant orange, radiant fiery ruby red and deep dark hues of mahogany brown. The assortment of colors is spectacular! This New England landscape, which appears to be endless miles of stunning and pristine countryside, is extraordinary!

We are viewing Mother Nature at its finest. These images are magnificent. I do not know enough words to describe this phenomenal beauty adequately, but I do know that it is absolutely fantastic to see such magnificent sights, and I am blessed to be sharing this experience with my mother. I pray this time in our lives will continue to be wonderful and we will keep these memories. I hope my writings will help us remember.

The bus passes over rivers and streams along the rocky Atlantic coastline, past the lakes, on its way to Portland's waterfront. The air is crisp, the breeze is mild, and the sun is brilliant. The bright blue sky is loaded with beautiful cumulus clouds floating through the air. Later, we traveled down the coast to the Maine Maritime Museum. There, we see antique boats, a large shipyard, and an extensive display of maritime posters.

For lunch we drive down a rocky promontory Five Islands Lobster in Georgetown for a lobster roll, a sandwich native to New England. The tender and delicious lobster meat is delicately seasoned, cooked, and served on a grilled, buttered bun, and it is delectable! Mom does not like to try different foods, but she agreed to take a bite of my lobster roll after I told her it was delicious. Her "little bite" became the remainder of my sandwich. No problem, I ordered another one and had it cut in half, and she ate half of that one, too. Mamma really enjoyed "our" lobster roll, and I am glad she did.

24: A Memory From The Past

When I was a little girl, Mamma always gave me the window seat so I could look out and see the world passing by. Now, many years later, she is an elderly lady who sits by the window to watch the passing scenes. Our positions have changed, but our outlooks are the same as we continue to view our passing world together and enjoy every mile of our journey.

The bus is steadily rolling along the highway when Mom seems to be observing a small group of people fishing in boats near the shore. Suddenly, she turns, nudges my arm, and says to me, "I used to go fishing at a place like that!" Immediately, I look out of the window and turn toward her. Now, my mother has my complete attention, and she continues to tell me, "When I lived in Connecticut, I went fishing all the time. I enjoyed fishing and caught a lot of fish, too."

"Yes, yes, you certainly did, Mamma," I responded and continued to smile. Oh, the joy I felt hearing what she said. God had answered my prayers. What my mother just said to me made this entire trip so meaningful. She remembered that she lived in Connecticut and recalled a specific location.

We sat in complete silence for a long time. I wanted to savor the joy of what she had said. For miles, we continued to look out of the window, enjoying the

Traveling Down the Road With Grace

beautiful autumn scenery while passing by the stately city of New Haven, Connecticut. That afternoon, the tour bus arrived in Mystic, home of the historic Mystic Seaport, the nation's leading maritime museum dedicated to the golden age of seafaring.

When the bus stopped at the next location, we were ready to stretch our legs and walk about as we explored this noteworthy town. Mamma and I locked arms and casually strolled along the ocean-lined pathways. We viewed the impressive 'tall ships,' later passed an art gallery, and decided to go in. There, I met the friendly proprietor and told her that we wanted to purchase a painting that was reflective of the region. We browsed through the aisles, looking at artwork. I asked my mother to select a portrait that would remind her of this trip. After looking for just the right picture, Mom turned and handed me a relatively small yet attractive painting, and she said to me, "I like this one. I saw this yesterday."

"Yes, you did," I replied to her, and I took the painting to the register to purchase it. "We did see this lighthouse," I realized as I continued to smile and remember the occurrence. Yes, and Mamma remembered it, too! The portrait was beautiful. It was small, yet so significant! We saw it off the Atlantic coast yesterday! "Wow! This is better than I expected," I thought to myself.

Traveling Down the Road With Grace

Now, for the remainder of the story. The painting that my mother selected was an image of the Nubble Lighthouse. Let me tell you more about this particular lighthouse. First of all, we learned that it is a classic example of an American lighthouse with a tremendous amount of history surrounding it. This portrait will hold personal history for us because it was a scene my mother and I had seen during our sightseeing tour in Maine, and my mother remembered it!

Of course, I definitely wanted to purchase the painting. This beautiful work of art became even more special when the art gallery proprietor told us that she knew the artist personally and proceeded to tell us a bit of his background. She told us that the seventy-plus-year-old artist started painting late in his life after being diagnosed with Alzheimer's. I believe his beautiful portrait was an inspiration for my mother when she later became a budding artist.

Traveling Down the Road With Grace

25: The End Of Our New England Tour

The famous English author Mr. Geoffrey Chaucer once said, "All good things must come to an end." I whispered those exact bittersweet words to my mother when I smiled and kissed her cheek. It was evident that our New England journey was winding down when we saw the end of the once glorious autumn season gradually fading away.

Most of the trees that were previously loaded with brightly colored leaves now have limbs that are nearly bare. A chilly gust of wind blows the few remaining leaves through the air as they float around and finally land on the ground. The morning air feels much cooler, and "sweater weather" now requires jackets and coats. The tour bus continues to roll through the countryside as we head to our final destination before returning to Boston.

When the bus approached the picturesque harbor of Kennebunkport, Maine, I immediately thought, "WOW! This little haven is breathtakingly beautiful!" Later, we passed an enormous manor surrounded by security vehicles, and the tour guide informed us that we were passing the Bush Compound. We learned it was the summer home for the families of George H.W. and their son, George W.

We had time to wander about this picturesque town on a walking tour. We learned some of its history during our visit to this distinctive town located by the sea. In the 1660s, the area developed a great ship-building industry, and on a regular basis, masted ships and schooners traveled along the Kennebunk River as they headed to the Atlantic Ocean. Wealthy sea captains built extravagant mansions, and many of those buildings have been preserved. Today, several of the stately manors have been converted into attractive inns for the many visitors who arrive every year. Mom and I strolled down the streets of this charming little hamlet, holding hands while we walked down the stoned streets, and it felt as though we were walking back in history.

We wandered into one of the boutiques, and while we browsed through the shop, Mamma noticed an attractive jacket that she liked. She tried it on and smiled. The stylish, short coat was a nice fit, and the color looked good on her. "Great!" I thought, "This can be a souvenir for her, a beautiful bright golden-colored jacket to keep her warm, and she obviously liked it very much." Mamma smiled again when the clerk handed her a bag containing another memory from our trip.

Later, the group of tourists returned to Boston, and that evening, the entire group and our guide

Traveling Down the Road With Grace

celebrated our last dinner together as we dined on whole Maine lobsters with all of the trimmings. Many of the travelers had "gussied up" for our final evening meal. A few glasses of wine clicked with biddings of farewell. Some people talked about their favorite sights, and others told us about their plans for future travel. We exchanged our final farewells, and everyone seemed to have enjoyed the tour, especially Miss Grace and her daughter. We both learned another lesson: group travel works very well for both of us. I think we may do it again!

The next day, Mamma and I remained in Boston for our extra-scheduled day of relaxation before we returned home. I asked Mamma if she wanted to stay in and rest or go out and explore the city a bit more. She did not hesitate when she quickly responded, "Girl, Let's go!"

26: The "Springs"

We returned home after touring New England in the Fall, and we felt wonderful. Mamma and I were traveling again, and we wanted to continue, and that was exactly what we did. Early Saturday morning we left home and planned to enjoy a bit of Colorado's beautiful countryside. We traveled down Interstate 25 South, a corridor that runs parallel to the Rocky Mountain range.

Throughout our former lives, neither of us had lived in a mountainous region, and now that we do, we enjoy traveling alongside the mountains as often as we can. My mother likes seeing the snow on top of the hills and always reacts as if it were her first time! She happily exclaims, "There's snow on top of the mountains!" Even though I do not say it aloud, I share the same excitement when I see that scene. Yes, I admit, when I first saw that sight, I immediately snapped photographs of the views and sent them to some of my friends in Indiana.

The majestic Rocky Mountains are awesome, and images of those huge ranges always remind me of the lines from the well-known poem "The Creation," written by the renowned poet James Weldon Johnson.

***"And God walked and where he trod
His footsteps hollowed the valleys out
And bulged the mountains up."***

This image clearly personifies the magnitude of God, who walked, and His footsteps created enormous mountain ranges that stretched more than 20,000 feet toward the sky. What a mighty God! Of course, I realize that the poem is a perception of God, but I know that God is real. Those mountains are there, and I believe that God formed them. Perhaps that is why my mother and I appreciate seeing mountains so much. They are visual reminders of God's greatness here on earth!

We made a pit stop for lunch in Manitou Springs, the little "hippie dippy town," as we liked to refer to it. This region has great food and picturesque scenery. We enjoyed strolling through this very popular town, which is nestled so beautifully within the surrounding mountain ranges.

Legend says, "In 1859, a surveyor named Rufus Cable first saw the rocks jutting out over 300 feet high near Pike's Peak." He was so excited he said that this area was "a place fit for gods to assemble!" I imagine those who heard him repeated his statement and the rest of the story is history. The picturesque region took on its name and became a popular place to visit. The area is absolutely gorgeous! This portion of Colorado looks like a "wonderland of enormous rocks," and it is loaded with scenic mountain views. There is no charge nor entry fee to enter this area. As nature should be, it is free for all spectators to visit and appreciate one of Mother Nature's grandest attractions.

The Garden of the Gods is a natural creation of spectacular red rock formations. The eight miles of trails is home to the "Kissing Camels." The famous "Balanced Rock" is a spectacle that must be seen to believe. This huge 35-foot-high red rock stands on tippy toes and amazingly weighs 1.4 million pounds. There is the "Old Indian" and even more of the larger-than-life-sized characters.

My favorite "amazing work of rocks" is the park's rendition of Charles Shultz's "Snoopy" lying on his back, which is a delight for children of all ages, young and old. As unbelievable as they may appear, all of these formations were naturally, artistically designed. They are untouched by man's chisel and located in the shadows of Pike's Peak. Amazingly, Mother Nature is the artist who created all of these innovative rock formations!

28: Music & Dancing On The Mountains

My mother and I arrived at the Denver Union Station early one Friday morning, headed to Winter Park, Colorado. We boarded the westward-bound California Zephyr Amtrak train. We enjoyed the stunning scenery during our ride as the train rolled through the picturesque Rocky Mountain National Park. Large patches of beautiful, yellow wildflowers sprouted between the mountain ridges, loaded with aspen trees that were gently "quaking" in the mild breezes.

The engineer steadily reduced the speed of the train as it gradually climbed up the mountain, and we continued our ride through twenty-seven tunnels in thirty minutes while going through the mountains. The higher the train ascended, the more stunning the spectacular views appeared. We saw miles and miles of lofty and magnificent mountain ranges, surrounded by spectacular views of the skyline and brilliantly colored landscape.

Shortly before noontime, we headed toward the dining car for lunch. Walking on a moving train is not easy for strong and sturdy passengers, and it is a serious challenge for two elderly ladies like us! After swaying back and forth and wobbling through three of the jerking and continuously moving passenger compartments and two observation cars, we managed to remain on our feet. Finally, Mamma and I arrived in the diner. Unfortunately, we were told that we had to wait at least an hour before we could have lunch.

In the meantime, there was no available place to wait. Our only option was to make a reservation, return to our previous seats, and wait for our names to be called. We wobbled back through the utterly full observation car, and when we passed a young man who remembered us from previously passing by, he automatically stood up and offered Mamma his seat, and the fellow sitting next to him did the same for me. What an unexpected surprise!

I offered them lunch as a gesture of appreciation for their much-desired seats. They graciously declined my offer, and we courteously accepted their seats. "Wow," I exclaimed when I realized we had been given choice seats while waiting for our lunch reservation. The coveted spaces in the observation car have large windows from the ceiling to the floor and offer panoramic views of the passing scenery.

I noticed Mamma was smiling when she saw the beautiful mountain views from the large windows. Today is special because my mother and I are sharing this wonderful experience together, and this is our first train ride together through Colorado. I have frequently traveled on this route and have always thought, "Mamma would enjoy seeing all of these beautiful mountain views," and today, Thank God, we are sharing this delightful journey together.

"Joann, party of two! Your table is ready," suddenly blared from the loudspeaker. We wobbled back through the cars to reach the dining car; this time, seats were available. We enjoyed our meal and chatted for a while, and soon, the train was pulling into the Winter Park, Colorado, terminal. "That was great timing," I thought as we swayed back and forth to our seats in the passenger cars.

When we arrived at our destination and departed the train, we headed to our lodge and enjoyed a restful evening. This trip is extra special since we also have tickets to attend a two-day jazz festival. I remember how much my mother enjoyed listening to music when I was a young girl. She played her records of some of the musical greats like Ella Fitzgerald, Louis Armstrong, Miles Davis, and Billie Holliday, to name a few. I thought if she enjoyed them, perhaps she would also enjoy listening to some of today's performers, live and in the mountains too. This event will be an enjoyable experience for both of us!

The next day, we attended the Annual Winter

Park Jazz Festival. The opening act was Mary Louise Lee, and she was fantastic, as her soft and mellow voice poured out beautiful ballads. The next performer was Larry Graham, who sounded great and had electric energy, performing "Hot Fun in the Summertime." As time passed with hours of non-stop music and more outdoor sun than we needed, I thought my mother might be ready to leave. I gently nudged her and whispered, "We can go now."

Mamma quickly responded, "Oh, no, let's stay!" "Well," I thought, "Good! She must be **really** enjoying herself." We both continued to have a good time, listening to all of George Benson's nonstop, dynamic songs. I am so glad my mother wanted to stay because his finale was fantastic. She taught me a lesson today! I learned that my mother is much stronger than I thought and can last longer than I could imagine.

The second day of the jazz festival was more exciting than the first. We returned to the outdoor theater to enjoy the remainder of the concert. Would you believe my Mamma was dancing in the aisle? Yes, she was! It all started when she was sitting in her chair, clapping her hands, twisting, and turning in her seat. Mamma was enjoying herself, and unexpectedly, a young man walked toward her and, with utmost courtesy, extended his hand toward her, a gentleman's request for a dance partner. Mamma seemed surprised at first, but she graciously accepted the invitation, and the two of them proceeded to dance in the aisle. She was so happy to be dancing, and it was apparent, too.

The lady enjoys dancing and swaying to the music. Sometimes, she can be a bit of a "show off" with her "smooth moves." Although they did not look like Fred and Ginger, Miss Grace and her dance partner put on an entertaining performance in the aisle, and all the while, their nearby audience encouraged them by clapping and cheering during their performance. Who would have imagined my eighty-year-old mother attending a jazz concert in the mountains of Colorado and dancing in the aisle? What a time we had!

The next day, we boarded the train for the return trip home. After going through the last of the tunnels, we could see the outline of the "Mile High City," Denver, Colorado, miles away. We definitely do not see sights like this every day, but we enjoy seeing them now, especially when Mamma and I are so happy together. God is blessing us abundantly to be able to share all of these wonderful experiences together.

29: He Knew!

When tickets for **Memphis, The Musical**, went on sale, I immediately purchased a ticket and obtained an excellent seat. Months later, Mamma was living with me, and the play had come to town. I thought she would enjoy attending the performance, also. Fortunately, I was able to purchase an additional ticket for the tremendously popular presentation, but unfortunately, our seats were far apart.

On the evening of the performance, we arrived at the theater early and sat next to each other using the ticket for the closest seat to the stage and the currently vacant seat next to it. I was prepared to move when the person arrived to claim the seat that I had temporarily borrowed.

When the owner of that seat showed up, he surprisingly insisted that I remain in his seat. He told us he had seen the play several times, and he refused to take the seat! The gentleman explained that his daughter was in the production, and he came every week to support her. He graciously accepted my "further away" spot for that evening. As a matter of fact, he adamantly refused to take his assigned seat so that I could remain seated next to my mother.

As he walked away, I thought, "What a wonderful father and a blessing for us because I really did not want my mother sitting alone during the performance." Thankfully, we accepted his offer, knowing Mamma would be more comfortable with me nearby. I gave her a hardy 'High 5!' as we relaxed in our seats, ready for the show to begin.

What a show it was! This performance was based on a story about a disc jockey, Dewey Phillips, one of the first white disc jockeys in Memphis, Tennessee, to play Black music in the 1950s. He made a dynamic impact in the music world during that time. Many doors for Black entertainers in that southern city busted wide open as the soulful songs rapidly spread like Wildfire across our country. It was HOT! The list of Black artists from Memphis is long and includes musical greats like Al Green, Junior Wells, Isaac Hayes, Sam & Dave, Koko Taylor, and more.

This production stirred warm memories for my Mamma. I think it was reminiscent of the era when she and her friends had "rent parties," and this music was similar to the songs that blasted from their record players playing those 78 RPM vinyl records "back in the day." I think Mamma remembered a few of those tunes, too! Throughout the show, I watched her from the corner of my eye as I was checking her out! I wanted to see her reactions to all of that invigorating, soul-stirring music.

The lady was dancing in her seat and twisting from side to side. She was turning her shoulders, bobbing her head, and clapping her hands! Yes, Indeed, everyone near could see that Mamma was having a good time, and she was not alone, either. Many others were "dancing in their seats!" It was apparent that the entire audience enjoyed the performance, according to the tremendous applause and repeated encores that the cast received.

As we were leaving the theater, still under the influence of all of that electrifying rock and roll music, it dawned on me that this was the first time my mother and I had been to the theater together and we both enjoyed it tremendously! "No wonder we were able to sit next to each other and enjoy the music, the memories, and the love," I thought to myself, "What a special event this was. It was such a blessing to share an enjoyable evening with my mother at this time in our lives. For all of the occasions that we missed together during my childhood, God was giving us so many wonderful opportunities to share them now. These are times we treasure every occasion to replenish our love. God is a restorer, and He is so good!

Traveling Down the Road With Grace

    I scanned the audience again while looking for "the kindhearted father." I wanted to tell him how much my mother and I enjoyed our seats together. Although I did not see him again, God assured me that he knew. Mamma and I walked out of the theater arm in arm after having a great evening! I was certain that God knew how much this evening would mean to us and I believe He arranged our seating. As we left the theater, I thought to myself, "Yes, He knew!"

Traveling Down the Road With Grace

30: The Theater, The Second Time

During Black History Month, we attended the play The Whipping Man. This dramatic presentation was completely different from the delightful musical we enjoyed before. The play begins at the end of the Civil War when Black slaves are being freed, and soldiers are returning home to their families throughout the South. Also, this is the time for the annual celebration of the Passover, the holiday commemorating the Hebrews' liberation from slavery in Egypt.

During the play, a young Confederate officer who had been severely wounded arrives home and finds his family's plantation in ruins and abandoned, except for two former slaves, Simon and John. The three men wait in the empty house for the other family members to return. Meanwhile, the men wrestle with their shared past, the bitter irony of Jewish slave-owning, and the reality of the new world in which they find themselves.

The sun sets on the last night of Passover as Simon, having adopted the religion of his masters, prepares the Seder. He plans to observe the ancient celebration of the liberation of the Hebrew slaves from Egypt, noting the parallels to his current situation. This tradition does not pacify the severe pain of being enslaved, and deep-buried secrets from the past arise as the play comes to its shocking climax.

It was too late when I realized that this was not a performance that my mother and I were prepared to see, and it was not a pleasant experience for either of us. I cannot imagine the incidents that my mother may have encountered throughout her lifetime as an African American woman who lived through times in this country when racial injustices were highly prevalent, as a result of the shadows of slavery and racial discrimination. We both had trouble with segments of the play, and afterward, I tried to discuss the performance with her, but she did not want to talk about it.

The previous production we attended, **Memphis, the Musical,** was so delightful and entertaining that I was too anxious to take Mom to another performance. Had I done a bit of research, I am sure we would not have seen this performance. Afterward, I realized that the title of the play, its theme, and the setting should have given me strong indications that attending this play would not be a pleasant experience for us.

I have learned a valuable lesson. As my mother sometimes says, "Bought sense is the best sense in the world!" Let me be the first to admit, "I bought a bit of sense for the price I paid for those theater tickets and the discomfort the performance caused both of us! Now, let us move forward. Thank you!

31: My Cousin, Bobby (March, 2016)

One afternoon, I received a phone call from a relative telling me that my cousin, Bobby, had passed away. The news was shocking especially since he was a young fellow who maintained such a healthy lifestyle. Bobby was the only son of my mother's sister and a favorite among our family members.

Since I knew Mamma was so fond of Bobby and hearing the news of his passing would be upsetting, I delayed telling her until I felt it was a suitable time to give her the news. I even thought, "Perhaps she will not remember him. After all, it has been a long time since she has seen him, and she tends to forget some things occasionally." I did not know when or how to tell her, so I prayed and asked God to let me know and He did.

The following morning, after we finished breakfast, I refilled our coffee cups and sat very close to her. I thought this was the time to inform her about Bobby. I said, "Mamma, I need to tell you something." She turned toward me and asked, "What is it, Baby?" I slowly continued, "Bobby passed away yesterday." Immediately, she stopped and looked directly into my eyes, and she asked, "Are you talking about Bobby, Anne's son?" I replied, "Yes." She started to cry, and so did I. "Yes, Mamma remembered him," I realized as I put my arms around her shoulders and gently hugged her, and we continued to cry together in each other's arms. We both know that losing someone you love is a heart-aching pain like none other. Now Bobby's mother, his wife, sister, children, and the rest of our family members will also know, again. I knew my mother had not seen her nephew in a while, but she remembered him! I also learned that we would attend his funeral services.

"ALL ABOARD!" We heard the conductor's call when we settled in our seats on the Zepher train headed to Chicago, Illinois. We always enjoyed our train rides, but this journey was not pleasant as we left to attend the funeral services for one of our favorite relatives.

Bobby was an ordinary fellow who lived an extraordinary life! His family loved him, his friends admired him, his neighbors appreciated him, his church members respected him, and his co-workers valued him.

I remember Bobby when he was a little fellow, and we were young children growing up together. He has always been a great guy, kindhearted and helpful. Throughout the years, the two of us were good buddies. As a youngster, he would continuously go out of his way to help others, and when he became an adult, that trait flourished with him even more. His passing was a tremendous loss for our family. We loved him and will always miss him.

  The admiration for my cousin was evident by the vast number of people who attended his service. The church was filled to capacity! Many people were in line to speak about their relationships with him and share his numerous contributions throughout the years with the audience. During his life, Bobby offered so much to so many. The young people spoke of occasions when he gave his time and resources to help them. Since he and his wife were admirable parents for their three children, he was a natural mentor for the youngsters and adolescents in their congregation. Some of the elderly people shared instances of the frequent times he had done tasks from maintenance repairs to purchasing groceries. The funeral service lasted much longer than planned because so many people wanted to share their memories and thoughts about his wonderful life!

  "WOW," I thought as Mamma and I sat in the pew with our family, "What a commentary for an exceptional life, well lived!" Bobby loved God, our family, and his fellow man. He was a devoted husband and a dedicated father. This young man was a caring son for his elderly mother, a dutiful brother to his younger sister, and a faithful church member of his congregation. He was well-loved by his family members and his numerous friends. Bobby was not a saint, but he lived a righteous life.

Of all the contributions that my cousin had made throughout his lifetime, the one that I thought was the most amazing was his final gift. He was an organ donor. Because he was young, a nonsmoker, and never drank alcohol, he was a multiple organ donor. Even in death, this young man was an incredible blessing to many individuals, and his final gifts were reflections of the extraordinary life that he had lived.

Yes, his sons are organ donors, too, and my mother and I are also, as well as many other family members and friends. I pray that everyone who reads my cousin's story will discuss this situation with their family members and consider organ donation.

32: Friendships And Baskets

My mother's best friend, Miss Correne, is a delightful lady and they have been friends longer than they can remember. The two of them met years ago and have remained friends since. Some time ago, Miss Correne's husband passed, and she moved to Charleston, South Carolina, to live with her daughter. A few years later, Mamma's husband passed, and she moved with me. Through the years, the ladies have maintained their long-term friendship through weekly telephone conversations that sometimes last for hours. They constantly repeat incidents that occurred in their former lives that usually begin with, "Do you remember when?"

Mamma and I realized that her best friend would not fly under any circumstances, and we know that my mother really enjoys flying across the country. We boarded a plane and headed to Charleston, South Carolina, to visit Miss Correne. This trip would give me an opportunity to spend some time with my long-time friend who also lives in the area. We arrived, and my mother and her best buddy reunited. They were so delighted to see each other after a long absence. First, they hugged each other, and Mom said to Miss Correne, "Girl, you look so good!" Her friend denied the compliment and immediately responded, "Oh, no I don't, but **you** sure do!" They continued their delightful barrage of compliments as they kindheartedly bantered back and forth on the subject of "looking good!"

Finally, the ladies smiled and nodded their heads in agreement. I smiled and adamantly responded, "Both of you are very attractive ladies. You look in the mirror!" After I made that statement, the compliments ceased for a while. Then the best buddies continued to smile and laugh, as they talked about bits and pieces of incidents from their past years. My mamma just had to have the last word and she hastily blurted, "Girl, you really do look good!" Both of them burst into another round of laughter!

Their delightful verbal sparring ended, and they shifted gears when they started conversations about their "good old days." The ladies talked about things they should not have and softly uttered topics that were taboo to anyone but them as they used their cleverly **coded** forms of conversation.

They finished each other's sentences, which were punctuated with repeated outbursts of laughter! The girlfriends' clever dialogues were so amusing and entertaining. Miss Correne and Mamma's relationship is a perfect example of genuine friendship. Although they had not seen each other in many years, they acted as though their last day together was yesterday. I understand because the same is true with my friend, Jacqueline. We have not seen each other in several years but have stayed closely connected via telephone conversations. Every few years, we seem to reunite, and our friendship has not diminished one bit. She lives in Charleston and knows that my mother and I were visiting that region, and we wanted to spend time together.

While Miss Corrine and Mamma spent the day together, Jacqueline and I headed to a very special place nearby, Mount Pleasant, South Carolina. The residents in the area have created an enormous market for sweetgrass baskets, which is a treasured history lesson that is deeply rooted in this part of the country. The beautiful baskets represent the very prominent Gullah/African American culture in Charleston and their makers regularly share the history of their craft.

Making Sweetgrass Baskets has been part of this community for centuries. The tradition was brought to the region by slaves who came from West Africa, and it is one of the oldest art forms of African culture in the United States. This unique skill has been passed from generation to generation. The tightly woven and very well-made containers were originally crafted for the practical use of collecting rice and cotton from the fields on the slave plantations.

Throughout the history of our country, there have been countless stories of African Americans with the inherent ability to take "nothing" and create "something!" The "something" is great and wonderful and becomes extremely valuable throughout time. This trait is exquisitely woven within the sweet grass baskets, which are made of **palmetto, long pine needles, and bulrush, that flourish abundantly in the area.** Amazingly, what was once used as a functional item for work has now developed into a valuable object of art. The prices of these beautiful artifacts range from less than a hundred dollars to more than several thousand dollars. The sweet grass baskets are like friendships. Both increase in value as time goes by and when they are woven together well, they will last for a long, long time and will become better with time.

33: History Of The Blues

When summer arrived, my mother and I headed to Memphis, Tennessee, which has the distinction of being one of the four largest cities that sits on the edge of the mighty Mississippi River. This unique multicultural city is rich in southern culture. The area is well known for its delicious bar-b-que and some of the best blues singers ever. We went to one of those "rib joints" and devoured a batch of delicious ribs.

Afterward, we sashayed down Beale Street and strolled to the beat of the crooning of Riley B. King, also known as Mr. B. B. King, the "Beale Street Blues Boy," a nickname that was attached to him when he was a young DJ on the radio. The loudspeakers along the street blared out a recording of one of his popular renditions; The **Thrill is Gone.** Hearing that song while strolling down the world-famous street, reminded me of an evening in Birmingham, Alabama, several years ago. I attended his concert when B. B. King crooned his songs to the packed audience of blues lovers, and we all responded with roars of applause and numerous encores.

This area of the South has the honor of being the "birthplace of the blues." During this visit, we

Traveling Down the Road With Grace

discovered additional information on the history of this music. We learned that during the Civil War, an isolated group of tired African American soldiers sat by the campfires late at night. The "war weary" men sang their soulful versions of songs about their battles while someone in the background would moan and groan a few words as a refrain. The dark-skinned soldiers, who were separated from the other warriors, sang recollections of their battles. Their music included the chants and hollers they remembered from working in the cotton fields. Some people believe they even incorporated some of the rhythms and chants from their African heritage and culture as they recollected their dreadful past experiences.

This distinctive music was a predecessor to the Delta blues, which was later heard in "Juke Joints," the small shanty-like buildings that functioned as social clubs. Once the blues was born, the music grew and rapidly spread across the area. Numerous great musicians came from this part of the country, such as Robert Johnson, Howling Wolf, and Muddy Waters, and the list grows and includes many lesser-known musicians and singers.

In search of new adventures, we headed down Highway 61 and passed Highway 49. This location is said to be the site that inspired the event about the notorious blues guitarist, Robert Johnson, who had a burning desire to become a great blues musician. The story is told that he was instructed to take his guitar to the crossroad at midnight, and there he supposedly met the devil, who took his instrument, tuned it after playing a few songs, and returned it to Johnson, giving him mastery of it in exchange for his soul.

This tale also includes an account by Son House, a famous blues performer, and a very close contemporary of Johnson. Son claimed that before Johnson achieved fame, the performer had previously been considered just an average harmonica player but a terrible guitarist. One night he suddenly disappeared from Clarksdale, Mississippi. Rumors began to spread throughout that country town that Johnson died on August 16, 1938, and he was the suspected victim of a deliberate poisoning at the age of twenty-seven.

On September 26, 1937, a tragedy occurred involving Bessie Smith, one of the greatest blues singers of her era. It was reported that she was critically injured in a terrible automobile accident while she and her entourage were driving on Highway 61 between Tennessee, and Clarksdale, Mississippi . According to the report, the nearest hospital refused to accept a person of color as a patient. She was taken to a different hospital that was much further away, and she died the next day at the Afro-American Hospital, which was later renamed the

Riverside Hotel, in Clarksdale, Mississippi. The site of that hotel is a historic marker on the Mississippi Blues Trail .

As we continued to travel through the area, we found our way to Delta Road, also known as Blues Alley. We had lunch at a restaurant known as **Ground Zero Blues Club**, which was a name chosen because Clarksdale, Mississippi has been historically referred to as "Ground Zero" for the blues. This blues club is owned by one of my favorite actors, Mr. Morgan Freeman, and his friend, the mayor of the city. "Now," I said to myself, "today I can sharpen my #2 pencil and scratch off another item listed on my bucket list." After listening to some genuine "down home" blues and dining on a batch of delicious fried green tomatoes and catfish, Mamma and I walked around the quaint little town for a while and enjoyed the nostalgia of a bygone era.

As we were riding down the back roads through Tennessee, we saw enormous fields loaded with hefty plants that had large, white blooms. My mother immediately recognized the crop. It was cotton that was growing on acres and acres of farmland that we passed. I guess seeing all of those cotton fields reminded Mamma of the times when she and some of her siblings picked cotton years ago. She described their back-bending labor in the burning hot sun, all day long. From what she told me about their experiences of picking cotton "back in the day," I understand why she and most of her relatives left the South as soon as they could purchase a one-way ticket up north.

Further down the road, we saw a couple sitting next to their parked truck, which was loaded with lots of big boxes and there was a large, handwritten "for sale" sign posted nearby. Once again, my Mamma immediately spotted the produce being sold and recognized it as, "new crop sweet potatoes." New and fresh they were. The entrepreneurs told us they dug them up early that morning and some of the sweet potatoes still had bits of red dirt on them. We bought a box, for the price of $10.00, why not? We continued our sightseeing excursion as we proceeded to explore miles of the rural backroads. Later, we returned to the city, after traveling throughout the picturesque countryside.

In Memphis, we visited the newly remodeled National Civil Rights Museum, which displays the history of the Civil Rights Movement from the 17th century to the present time. The museum consists of historical artifacts, exhibits, films, interactive media, and oral histories. It was built in 1991 to honor the memory of Dr. Martin Luther King's life and legacy. This dynamic civil rights leader, who was assassinated

Traveling Down the Road With Grace

on April 4, 1968, the direction of the history of America changed for minority people across our country. He came to Memphis to join the struggle with the city's sanitation workers on strike for increased wages and better working conditions. Dr. King led the march to lend his support to the workers' cause. We discovered a lot of history traveling down those dusty roads in Memphis, Tennessee.

34: Motor City Music And Memories

Some of my family members and friends advised me to take a temporary break from my caregiving responsibilities. I finally took their advice and planned to visit my goddaughter, Phyllis, for a weekend in Detroit, Michigan. Since I had not been there in years, I was looking forward to a visit to the "Motor City." Phyllis picked me up at the airport, and we went to the Motown Hitsville Museum on West Grand Boulevard, where we spent the remainder of the day at the musical empire that Barry Gordy created.

As founder of Motown Records, Mr. Gordy brought a sound to American music that endured the changes of time. He accomplished what many people thought could never be done. This multi-talented musical mogul put Black music into millions of white Americans' homes, by helping numerous artists to gain the acceptance of their music throughout the entire world. His determination and perseverance opened numerous doors for a host of successful African American record executives, producers, and musicians.

All of the songs that were written and released from "Hitsville USA" were the most enduring and popular music of our time. It is astonishing that even today, many of those songs are continuously played as the background music for movies and commercials. The words and music are still recognizable and frequently remembered by generations decades later. Those entertainers were considered some of the best in the industry with the quality of their songs, synchronized choreography, and extraordinary styles of dress.

It was decades ago when we danced to the hits of the Marvelettes, Gladys Knight, and the Pips, Diana Ross and the Supremes, Marvin Gay, (Little) Stevie Wonder, Michael Jackson and the Jackson 5, Smokey Robinson and the Miracles, Martha Reeves and the Vandellas at our basement parties and sock hops. Decades later, we still bobbed our heads and tapped our feet to those hits at our high school class reunions.

Visiting the Motor City and touring Hitsville, USA, sparked memories of my teenage era when the girls dressed in the very popular and fashionable felt 'poodle' skirts with bobby socks and Jacqueline shoes while carrying a matching 'bucket bag.' This was the classic outfit of the well-dressed high school girls of that era. The fellows donned their attire for "cool dudes" with their bright-colored shirts neatly tucked into their stiffly starched jeans, which were belted at their waists. Of course, we had to "dress the part" as well as know all of the words of the popular songs while we danced to the tempo of the music. Our high school and college days were filled with the sounds of the marvelous Motown music that blared from our record players and transistor radios during a period in time that seems like eons ago.

It was amazing that one man's dream, plus a loan of a few hundred dollars from his family, could expand and one day increase into a multi-million-dollar business, which speaks volumes of praise and admiration on behalf of Berry Gordy and African American entrepreneurship during his time. The success he obtained in a few years was simply incredible as his vision grew into phenomenal proportions when he created millionaires among so many vocalists and musicians. Motown Hitsville Museum represents the significance of Black music throughout the world.

During dinner that evening, I shared a bit of personal Detroit musical history with Phyllis. I told her about the time I first heard Aretha Franklin sing in a live performance. Being an active member of our Baptist Church in Gary, Indiana, I was selected as one of the teenage delegates to attend the National Baptist Church Convention of America in Chicago, Illinois. The minister for the evening was Rev. C.L. Franklin, Pastor of New Bethel Baptist Church in Detroit, Michigan, and he preached a dynamic sermon that evening. Before her father preached, Aretha Franklin sang a soul-stirring rendition of Thomas Dorsey's great gospel song, "Precious Lord." The immense audience was astonished when we heard the young, sixteen-year-old Aretha sing!

That was years ago, and I remember her dynamic performance. Of course, she received a standing ovation and more! There was an abundance of shouting and praising the Lord! Young Aretha was a singing sensation that evening in Chicago, Illinois. Little did I know, as an adolescent church girl, I sat in the audience, enjoying the melodic voice of the world's future "Queen of Soul!" with a few thousand Baptist people.

The next day my goddaughter and I visited the Charles H. Wright Museum of Africa, filled with impressive and informative exhibits. There we viewed an outstanding display of beautiful African American quilts, which was an unexpected pleasure, especially since quilting is my favorite hobby. That showcase was the first and only "African American Quilting Exposition" I ever attended. The quality of the quilts on display at the museum was exceptional, which is an indication that the quilters were masters. Attending the quilt show was a rare and unexpected pleasure.

The Detroit experience was revitalizing, informative, and inspiring. I had a wonderful weekend

Traveling Down the Road With Grace

in the Motor City. All went well, but I missed my Mamma. The brief break was good for us, and when we shared our *return hugs,* I knew Mamma had missed me, too. The weekend away was a good experience for both of us. We learned a valuable lesson: caregivers need to take an occasional break, and the person being cared for needs the same. "Absence makes the heart grow fonder!"

35: A Day Of Thanksgiving

We arrived at Denver International Airport, this time headed to Dallas, Texas, to celebrate Thanksgiving Day with our family. While we waited in the boarding area for our flight, my name was called over the speaker. "Oh, my goodness," I immediately thought, "I hope our flight has **not** been canceled!"

Fortunately, it was not, I was told when I went to the counter. The attendant informed me that we had been upgraded to first class! What a bonus blessing for our holiday trip. "Being a frequent flyer has benefits," I told Mamma as I smiled while we stood in line with the first group of passengers to board the plane.

Once we were on board, we settled in our large and comfortable seats and took out our headphones and iPods, which were filled with songs by our favorite artists like "Sassy" Sarah Vaughn, Ray Charles, Sam Cooke, Mahalia Jackson, Etta James, Nina Simone, and many of the "back in the day" entertainers. While traveling, we usually listen to our music, relax, and enjoy the flight. Music revives many good memories for both of us. Occasionally, a current artist or two is included in our collections, but we tend to appreciate those "oldies but goodies" more. Suddenly, smiles appear on our faces and a bit of head bobbing and foot tapping just might occur. After a few hours of hearing those soul-stirring and revitalizing melodies, our flight is about to end, and we put away our items to prepare for the landing.

We exited the plane and stepped onto the jetway. Mamma and I walked close to a wheelchair assistant who was standing nearby. He looked at my mother and said, "Ma'am, I have a wheelchair for you." She immediately stopped, looked directly at him, and replied, "Oh, no, you don't! It must be for somebody else because I can walk!" Afterward, she sashayed past the attendant and his wheelchair as she proceeded up the runway while swiftly walking toward the terminal, and she added a bit more sass with each step. She continued to walk up the ramp with her finest version of **Miss Grace's Strut**. "That's my Mamma," I said to myself with a smile as we proceeded to the luggage claim and waited for our bags to arrive on the carousel.

We were so happy when we arrived in Dallas, the hometown of my son, daughter-in-law, and three granddaughters. It is always good to visit our family, and they make the holidays so special for us. My daughter-in-law gives exceptional attention to the elderly folks, Mamma, and me. I frequently refer to her as a jewel since she is so precious to all of us.

Skylar, our oldest granddaughter is "Miss Dependable." We can always count on her. She is a mature and responsible young lady who makes good decisions and exhibits solid judgment. We are so proud of her academic achievements as she sets an excellent example for her sisters to follow.

My mother and I are delighted that she enjoys our cooking so much and she lets us know it. Skylar has told us on numerous occasions how much our version of a particular dish is the best that she has ever eaten. In her few years of life, I wonder how many variations of that particular dish she has tasted. Like her sisters, she is a pure delight.

Little Michele has grown up so quickly and is almost as tall as I am. Often, she says, "Grandma, you are the absolute best grandma in the whole wide world." When I remind her of her other grandmother, she quickly responds, "Oh, she is the absolute best Granny in the whole, wide world." The clever little rascal makes both of us feel so special.

Little Anna, our baby girl, is a tiny treasure and she is so precious. Mom and I constantly take turns, tenderly holding her as often as we can. When we gently wrap our arms around her, it seems as though we can actually inhale bits of her sweetness.

Traveling Down the Road With Grace

The girls grow so quickly. It is hard to believe that Michele and Skylar were once the size of Baby Anna. I imagine in a few years, their graduations will occur, later their weddings, and then their children. "STOP IT, Joann," I tell myself. I have accelerated time too rapidly! Let me appreciate the existing moments and enjoy the teenager, the young girl, and the tiny baby today and all the wonderful days to follow.

My grandchildren's' father is a wonderful daddy. He is a very good son and a dependable grandson. Surely there must be an advantage to being the only man in the house. He handles being surrounded by four females, six when Mamma and I arrive, quite well. He is always the boss; at least, we tell him so. He wants Mamma and me to relocate to Dallas. We average regular trips every few months so that we can participate in the activities of our young grand-girls as they grow up. Naturally, we want to be closer to the family and not just appear for special occasions. We really want to live closer to our children every day, and we plan to make the move, and it will come soon.

This Thanksgiving will be a huge celebration as my daughter-in-law's family and a few friends fill their home with more than thirty people. There will be loads of food, plenty of laughter, and an abundance of love as we celebrate this day of gratitude. What a blessing to be with plenty of family and friends to celebrate this season.

After dinner, the football fans gather in the media room to watch the game as they cheer and trash-talk. A handful of conversations remain around the dining room table to chat and sample a few of the delicious desserts. All of the children crowd into the den, which becomes their game room and immediately fills with music and laughter.

The day after Thanksgiving, I wake up early, have a cup of coffee, and enjoy the solitude of the early morning hour. I look out the window and see the rising sun as it appears. It is not climbing over the mountaintops as I usually see at home in Denver, but it is coming over the rooftops of the homes in the area. "Yes," I think to myself, "soon I will see the sunrise in Texas every morning when Mom and I call the Lone Star state our home. When we move to Texas, every day will be a day of thanksgiving, without all of the food."

36: To Grandmother's House

My mother was so happy when I told her that we would be moving to Texas soon. Since she enjoys warm temperatures year-round and really likes living in hot weather, she asks me almost every day, "When are we moving?" or "What day did you say we are leaving this cold town?" When the new year arrived, we started an ongoing search for a home located near our children.

We had an amazing realtor, and she was the answer to our prayers. She and I prayed when we first g
=met, and we continued to pray throughout the search for our new home. After numerous virtual observations and various showings, our relentless realtor successfully found a charming home for us and the location was the answer to our prayers.

Before we began our search, I prepared a list of "special requests" that I hoped our new dwelling would have. Amazingly, we obtained each item on the list! God answered our prayers, and we relocated to the Long Star state of Texas and currently live near our grandchildren. Although we can no longer see the sunset behind the majestic Rocky Mountains every day, we can spot a few hills nearby, and that adds to the beauty of the landscape.

Traveling Down the Road With Grace

Our grandchildren must ride "over a river and through a wooded area " to arrive at our home. I declare that we are now official grandmothers, according to the Thanksgiving Song, "Over the River and through the Woods!" We certainly enjoy living close to our family, especially the younger ones, and we are very happy. Mamma appreciates Texas' hot weather, and I am learning to adjust.

The people are friendly, at least most of them are. Even strangers will return a smile, and we just might even hear an occasional "Howdy, Folks, this is Big Tex!" when we visit the annual State Fair of Texas. Mamma has a garden in the backyard where she tends her flowers, and we planted several red rose bushes. A couple of honeysuckle bushes are starting to spread and climb the fence.

During the "warm weather days, The girls like to nestle close to their **Great Grace,** as they rock back and forth while the trio spends lazy afternoons eating ice cream and giggling as Mamma spins another one of her, "When I was a little girl   tales."

Occasionally, Mamma tells them about the times when she was growing up, and I hope one day, the girls will tell their children, "I remember when my Great-Grandmother told me   "

Traveling Down the Road With Grace

37: The Black History Tour

Now that we live closer to our children, we can do more family activities together. Our first combined event was a regional Black History Tour of Dallas, Texas. The all-day trip was informative and enjoyable. We learned so much about the people, culture, and lifestyles of the African American population in this region as it grew and developed throughout the past years.

From this local activity grew another one, a Family Black History Tour across the country. My son and daughter-in-law decided to visit some of the Black History Museums throughout the country, and they invited Mamma and me to share some of our personal experiences with them as we explored the museums. We gladly accepted their invitation, and both of us valued the opportunity to share such an enlightening activity with four generations of our family.

The world has changed tremendously through the years, and each generation has been affected. Our modern museums clearly reflect the vast amount of information and transformations that have occurred. Also, generational differences give us a broader perspective of our backgrounds and future. We hope our granddaughters appreciate the brave trailblazers as they continue to learn more about the bold experiences that our predecessors endured. Many doors that were previously closed to some people are now opened to all who are willing to soar to incredible heights.

Visiting the Black History museums was informative, yet sometimes uncomfortable, as we relived some of the dreadful incidents of our past. There were times when I had to step away from an exhibit to conceal and control the tears that automatically flowed. Occasionally, I noticed my mother sniffing a bit while wiping her eyes. In spite of the difficult episodes, the experience was beneficial.

As we were leaving the last museum, I recalled a quote by Maya Angelou: "You can't really know where you are going until you know where you have been."

Our trips included:

National Civil Rights Museum – Memphis, TN

The Legacy Museum: From Enslavement to Mass Incarceration – Montgomery, AL

The National Memorial for Peace and Justice– Montgomery, AL

The Civil Rights Institute – Birmingham, AL

We visited the town where my mother and I were born in Alabama. While we were there, we discovered that Mamma and I were delivered by the same midwife. The lady probably delivered most, if not all of my grandmother's children and her grandchildren who were born in that town.

Our family viewed the original Bible with pages that recorded the birthdates of my mother and all of her fifteen siblings. It was amazing to uncover documentation of our family history which was more than a century old. We discovered even more family history at the genealogy department in the town's library. This trip was an informative experience.

38: A Trip To Paradise

My mother's low energy level and her obvious weight loss were very distinct messages that we could not ignore. Our hearts were heavy, but we remained hopeful. Naturally, we were concerned, and the family continued to pray. While we were praying, God answered. My son, "the chief problem solver," responded in such a supportive way. Since his grandmother enjoys traveling, he planned a trip, and what a trip it was. He made arrangements for a vacation to the place called the Paradise of the Pacific, Hawaii. He believed the trip would be therapeutic for her and pleasurable for the family.

We visited the 50th and only state outside North America. We looked forward to spending a delightful week on the island with **Great Grace.** Each day was filled with exciting activities and adventures on the scenic island. To further enhance their appreciation of the beautiful and enchanting Hawaiian culture, our granddaughter's mother enrolled her young girls in a class that taught them to make Hawaiian leis, and they asked **Great-Grace** and me to join them. We watched the girls create beautiful floral necklaces designed with the gorgeous flowers from the islands.

Mamma was so happy, and I saw such joy in her smiles as she observed her great-granddaughters. Afterward, little Anna took her leis and put it around her great-grandmother's neck and gave her a big hug and a gentle kiss on her cheek! What a wonderful gift and such a display of, "genuine love." The young girl acted so spontaneously; I doubt if she was aware of the impact of her gesture. Little did the precious child know she had given her great-grandmother "a million-dollar kiss" and an enormous dose of therapy.

Every morning, my mother and I strolled along Waikiki beach. Afterward, we wandered into the surrounding gardens while slowly walking among the beautiful flowering plants and trees. Mamma admired the gorgeous array of tropical blossoms along the pathways, the elegant birds of paradise, the hibiscus, and the variety of beautiful orchids.

Some of these budding beauties had grown in her flower garden around her home in Alabama, and she identified a few of the tropical plants we had observed. I was delighted when Mamma let me know that she recognized some of the flowers and was very pleased when she remembered the names of so many of them! I smiled and thought to myself, "Mother Nature and my mother are very fond of each other!" We enjoyed our early morning strolls along the white sandy beaches surrounding the bright blue ocean and admired the numerous palm trees as they waved their branches amid the mild breezes. Walking around the tropical paradise, with brilliant blue skies and sunshine was her favorite thing to do. The sunrises and sunsets were spectacular. All of nature's beautiful and natural scenes were rejuvenating and restorative. This trip was revitalizing for my ailing mother. Her visit to the island offered tremendous doses of therapy, and every day, she relished the scenery, the pristine beaches, the ideal weather, an abundance of sunshine, and lush blue skies loaded with enormous, white, billowy clouds.

Oh, by the way, I tried several times to persuade Mamma to travel to Hawaii with me, and her response was always, "I don't want to go to Hawaii." One day, and only one time, her grandson asked her if she wanted to go to Hawaii with him, and immediately, she responded, "Oh yes! I do!"

Well, like I always say, God always gives us what we need when we really need it! We will always remember the gorgeous days we spent walking along the beautiful beaches in Hawaii with Great Grace. We experienced a bit of paradise here on Earth, and we were so happy to be able to share that glorious time together with her. We were so happy in Hawaii with Grace!

39: Sitting On The Back Porch

One Sunday afternoon, in the middle of July, Mamma and I returned home from church service and had dinner. After we finished our kitchen duties, I looked forward to a relaxing afternoon while watching a few good old western movies in the cooled air-conditioned den with the ceiling fan set on high. But **no**, not my Mamma! The lady wants to sit outside on the porch in the hot summer heat, and today is probably one of the hottest days of the year. Since the back porch has been screened, Mamma enjoys sitting there as she slowly rocks back and forth on her '**Great Grace Swing.**'

Today is the middle of July and it is HOT! Texas heat is no joke! Today's temperature is a sweltering one hundred-plus degrees even with the porch fan on the highest setting, and it just circulates additional heat, which does not seem to bother her at all, and she never complains about it! I believe my mother is immune to hot weather because she always acts as though exceptionally high temperatures do not affect her at all. She probably inherited that trait from her mother, my Big Mamma, because she was the exact same way.

Please understand. It is a pleasure to spend time with my Mamma, and I especially appreciate her sweet, loving spirit. I thank God for days like these. As a matter of fact, I pray God will permanently print this particular day in my mind so that I will always remember it. Because she wants to sit on the porch this afternoon in the heat, I will sit with her and try to smile as I wipe away all of the sweat!

After placing two tall glasses of ice water on the small table near us, I open my laptop and sit as close as I can to her as we slowly swing back and forth in the extremely hot temperature. Before I start typing, I catch a glimpse of Mamma from the corner of my eye. Honestly, there is no place I would rather be than here, next to my mother, on a beautiful day like today, and it is Sunday, too! I thank God for our many blessings. Slowly I inhale as I try to absorb bits of the atmosphere that is loaded with love and peacefulness while I sit close to my amazing Mamma on this extremely hot Sunday afternoon.

A few minutes later, I caught a glimpse of her from the corner of my eye and she is napping so peacefully. I suggest that she go into her cool-temperature bedroom and take a nap. She very quickly opens her eyes and immediately responds, "I wasn't sleeping, I was just resting my eyes!" She smiles at me, and I return her smile. I relax and continue to enjoy these precious moments. My mother is the most mild-mannered and peaceable person I know. Frequently, I wish I had inherited more of those traits from her. She is so kindhearted. Everyone who knows her loves her and I love her very much!

I have a strong suspicion of what the days ahead will offer when my mother is no longer with us. I pray God will replay scenes like today's as He allows me to simply close my eyes, smile, and remember us sitting on the back porch on Sunday afternoons, relaxing when we were so peaceful and very hot!

Mamma and I are blessed to have all of the wonderful days that the Master has given us to share with Him and each other. Now, I must move on. My laptop may not recover from a big batch of tears on this hot, hot summer day while sitting on the back porch, swinging back and forth on the "Great Grace Swing" with my Mamma.

40: Great Grace's Last Train Ride

Heavenly Father, we come before You seeking Your Grace and Mercy as You continue to watch over us while we are together. Thank You for protecting and keeping us. We are grateful that You have allowed us the privilege to take this journey. May we continue to have an enjoyable time.

Lord, I pray that we will travel safely and return home with renewed spirits and all praises for You. As we continue on this journey, may we represent You well, as children of the Most-High God. Thank You, Master, for giving my mother the energy and the strength to complete this great journey.

We pray that You will give us many lasting and wonderful memories that Michelle and I will forever keep in our hearts and cherish for the remainder of our lives. In Jesus's mighty name. AMEN and AMEN.

We prayed and God answered.

The three of us left Dallas traveling on the Amtrak train, the Texas Eagle. We climbed on board, assisting my mother as she carefully walked with her cane, and we very slowly took each step together. I gripped her arm a bit firmer when she mounted the steps, and afterward, we slowly walked to our assigned bedroom suite. Mack, as I affectionately call Michelle Grace, closely followed behind us with the overnight bags when we entered our very compact, but comfortable room. Grace's Trio, as I referred to us, arrived in Chicago the following day.

After checking into a downtown hotel for the evening, we returned to the train station the next morning to complete the remaining segment of our journey. It was a bright and pleasant mid-October day, and we looked forward to the second segment of our journey to Sacramento, California.

For the last decade, Mamma and I had become very familiar with these small-scaled bedrooms since the railroads are our preferred means to travel across the country. It did not take long for us to get comfortable as we prepared for the next couple of days of complete relaxation: sleeping, dining, and most of all, enjoying one of the most scenic railroad routes in America from our comfortable seats on the train. We were prepared to enjoy the time of our life.

"ALL ABOARD!" we distinctly heard the conductor's familiar call when the California Zephyr pulled out of the station in Chicago, Illinois. Grace's trio was visually exploring miles and miles of cornfields stretching across the country, loaded with

Traveling Down the Road With Grace

more cows than we cared to count and filled with numerous farmhouses and lots of red barns. We headed westward on this beautiful sunny day in the middle of the fall season.

The song "America the Beautiful" resonated in my mind as we traveled through the states of Illinois, Iowa, and Nebraska and finally reached Colorado. From the views surrounding the historic Denver Union Station, we caught a few glimpses of the magnificent "Mile High City," which was our former home a few years ago. For several fall seasons, Mamma and I had seen the Rocky Mountains, loaded with dazzling aspen trees, but never had we seen them like this. They appeared absolutely brilliant for their grand appearance on this particular occasion!

The California Zephyr continued to steadily rumble through Utah and Nevada as the brightness of the autumn landscape increased and magnified with such a vibrant display of red, orange, and golden leaves, blending so perfectly with enormous, bulbous white clouds. Autumn appeared to be spectacular! She was dressed in her finest fashions from head to toe. The season had shown up and was now showing out! I prayed that we would arrive at the peak of the beautiful fall season, and we had. When the train pulled into California, I thought, "WOW! What Hollywood does to its magnificent movies, Mother

Nature designs these beautiful scenic backgrounds for us to appreciate and enjoy."

My mother's health is gradually declining, and we sense she will not improve. This trip is very special for her, especially since she has always enjoyed traveling on trains. A bonus blessing for the grandmothers is to have Michelle with us. This is her first train ride, and naturally, she makes this journey extra special. She offers a load of assistance, but more importantly, her presence is an 'energy boost' for us. I believe young people generate positive energy for the elderly.

It did not take long for the three of us to comfortably settle in our "home" for the next two days and nights. Mamma watched her favorite movie, "The Green Book," between napping and viewing the scenes of the picturesque countryside that we were passing. Mack relaxed and donned her headphones while enjoying music and reading. Between glances at the beautiful passing views, I continued to type on my laptop while trying to describe the extraordinary scenes of Americana steadily passing by the windows as the train roars continuously on the railroad tracks. I smiled with pure joy between occasional glances at my two Graces.

This period of time is so peaceful and so comforting. I want to savor all of the sweetness that I can from these precious moments before they evaporate. "Yes! Life is good, and God is even better," I constantly remind myself as our train continues to travel down the rails. Realizing that "nothing is too hard for God," I continue to thank Him for giving my mother the strength to enjoy this journey with us.

"So far, so good," I constantly remind myself. Like David, there are times we must encourage ourselves! Mom appeared to be doing relatively well, but I know she is getting weaker. I also know she wanted to make this journey, and we know "With God, all things are possible!"

Mamma and I have been traveling together for more than half a century now. Of all the trains, planes, buses, and cars we have taken, this trip will have top billing among all our adventures. No one said it, and we did not have to; we all knew. I knew, Mack knew, and Mom did, too. This is my mother's last train ride!

Amazingly, not a single tear was shed. We have nothing to cry about while making this journey. We are happy and joyful and having a GREAT TIME. The joy of Jesus floods our souls, and there is absolutely no room for sadness or tears. There is only joy in our hearts as we celebrate this journey.

After a total of three days on the trains, we arrived in Sacramento, California. Since we were in the Capital of the state, we wanted to see the capital building and the tour would be a part of Mack's homework assignment. She was posing in all of the pictures with Mom, and she even danced a few steps around her Great Grace and turned her around tenderly as they did a little dance. Mom smiled and did a two-step with Mack. Oh, the joy I saw in their faces! Heaven smiled at us, and we smiled at each other as they smiled at the camera, and I took as many photographs as I could.

The pleasant weather was ideal for the three of us—the great-grandmother and grandmother, and our fourteen-year-old girl—to walk hand-in-hand through the adjacent 40-acre Capital Park. We strolled along the manicured grounds and admired the trees from around the world surrounded by sporadic historical monuments and statues. We were making history while we walked among history.

Before we left home, I remembered how the doctors had picked their words so gingerly as they gave me my mother's prognosis before we planned to travel. They skipped around that dreadful word. The physicians knew and they knew that I knew the total situation and its possibilities. They were kind and gentle with their recommendations and advice, but all the kindness and gentleness in the world cannot remove the sting of knowing that someone you dearly love is nearing the end of life. You know and you know that they know. How do you handle such a situation? What do you do? What do you say?

I can only tell you what I said. I said, ***"THANK YOU, FATHER!" Yes, and I told God, "THANK YOU" for all of His blessings.*** I thanked Him for all of the years He gave us together. I thanked Him for the loving family who supported us so thoroughly. I thanked Him for the abundance of trips He had provided. I thanked Him for the trials and tribulations we overcame! I thanked Him for all of the wonderful times He gave us. I thanked Him for the readers who are reading our story. Today, I am still thanking Him, and I will continue to thank the Master forever!

41: The Return Trip

It took three days for Grace's Trio to arrive in Sacramento, California, but only three hours to return home. When we boarded the aircraft to Dallas, Texas, it was a full flight, but we had seats near the front. Walking down the aisle with Mamma took some time since we had to assist her with each step, but the fellow passengers were patient and tolerant. No one complained nor commented about our extremely slow procession. When we reached the row of our seats, Mack climbed into the window seat, and afterward, we slowly assisted Mamma to the center seat. I followed and sat in the aisle seat.

We nestled Great Grace between the two of us while making her as comfortable as we could with a large and cozy shawl wrapped around her extremely frail, thin shoulders. Occasionally, we gently snuggled against her, and it felt so good to be close to her. From the corner of my eye, I saw Mack softly place an occasional kiss on her GreatGrace's cheek and Mom responded with a weak smile. We wanted to feel the love, embrace her spirit, and absorb all of the tenderness that we could. Mamma's responses let us know she wanted us close to her, also. The language of love whispers so softly but it is always clearly heard.

We were very comfortable, settled in our seats and soon Mom was napping peacefully. Mack put on her headphones, turned on her music, and opened a book to read. I decided not to listen to music during this trip. All I wanted to do was relax and reminisce. I looked out of the window across the aisle as the huge jet started to climb into the sky. When we were flying between the billowy clouds, my mind started to travel down memory lane.

I remember when my mother was a young woman, and I was her little girl. I thought Mamma was so wonderful and she was! She was such a beautiful lady, inside and out, with a pretty face, a friendly smile, and a delightful personality. She was a sharp dresser and liked to dress fashionably. Mom loved her family and her friends, and she liked to dance and have fun. Yes, I remembered, when she was young. Now, God has blessed us to still have her in our lives when she is elderly. She is still wonderful and beautiful and continues to dress well and looks good!

Mamma liked to dance! When I was a little girl, she danced with me. Through the years, I remember her dancing. She was in the center of the floor dancing at her 80th birthday party in that beautiful white lace dress, dancing and teaching the children how to do the "Twist." I saw her dancing at her coronation. Queen

Traveling Down the Road With Grace

Grace was twirling and turning with her grandson on the dance floor at the Senior Center.

On the mountains, at the jazz concert in Colorado, she danced in the aisle with the young fellow. Just a few days ago, she and Mack did a little dance in front of the capital in Sacramento, California and she was smiling and enjoying herself............ and that was the last thing I recalled. I must have dozed off for a while. Suddenly, I heard the pilot making his closing announcements, "Please fasten your seat belts! Would all passengers, prepare for landing!" The flight attendants were strolling down the aisle, making their final collections.

I noticed Michelle and her Great Grace were holding hands and smiling. When I glanced at Mamma, she smiled at me. The three of us were smiling at each other and God had smiled on us. Yes indeed! Grace's Trio, all three of us, were returning home together. Thank God, He answered our prayers.

42: The Message Of Love

The family knew my mother's time with us was gradually declining. God had spoken, "Mamma will leave us soon!" Late that evening, I pulled the large recliner next to her recently provided hospice bed and we laid as close as possible to each other, face to face. She was not able to verbally communicate yet she expressed her most powerful message ever. Time was passing, and the hour was late when she stretched her hands toward me and reached for my hands, and I placed my hands in hers. In the silence of the still and peaceful night, we held hands for a while.

Slowly and very gently, my mother continued to clasp my hands and gave me a soft squeeze. I smiled when my fingers replied with one soft touch to hers. She lightly responded twice, and I returned the touch two times. We gradually and progressively continued our hand squeezing symphony ever so gently and gradually. When she reached her final refrain, she held my hand as firmly as she could, and I lightly gripped her fingers as securely as I could.

After her last pause, I took her hands and held them tenderly near my chest while I kissed her fingertips. Although she never spoke a word, Mamma had delivered her final and most powerful message!

She completed her unspoken communication to her daughter, and I amazingly received every single syllable!

We loved each other so much that our hearts could communicate. She let me know that she loved me, and I let her know that I loved her. She replied by clasping my hand, "I LOVE YOU MORE!!!" She **never** spoke a single word. Our hearts delivered the passion of our spirits. The entire "Litany of Love" allowed His voice to speak from our hearts.

Miraculously, at such a time, when my mother embraced the end of her life, she was so strong, and she powerfully conveyed her final message to her daughter. Our Father loves us so much that He gives us the incredible ability to accomplish a miraculous achievement at such a time!

I had tried so many times to complete our book, which I had been writing for more than ten years about our journeys to various cities and keeping records of our travels and activities. Throughout the last decade, my writings were typed, scribbled, and written in many notebooks and on two laptops! When I finally compiled our story, I had written a few hundred pages.

Yet, I still could not complete **THE BOOK,** as I referred to our document before I knew it's title. Some strange and daunting feelings held me back from accomplishing the task. I could not conclude our story and after many failed attempts, now I understand why. My mother had to complete our journey! Mamma **never** murmured a word during her "last" night with me and yet she completed our book as she started her journey to eternity. When I glanced at the clock, I noticed it was a few minutes before midnight.

Her grandson and daughter-in-law were with me, and their prayers and presence were so comforting. God gave us such peace with the passing of Great Grace, as we will always remember her. Grace will always be in our hearts.

A ninety-three-and-a-half-year-old lady lived an amazing life. She literally succeeded in a world that was not designed for her to survive. Not only did she endure obstacles throughout her lifetime, but she also overcame all of them. This strong woman flourished, all the way to the end of her journey. With the Grace of God, Grace Rebecca Knight conquered her little corner of the world and completed her journey triumphantly! Mamma is gone now, and **Traveling Down the Road with Grace** is completed. May we continue to travel with my mother through the pages of our book.

THE END

Traveling Down the Road With Grace

**Bonus Episode:
Prior to GreatGrace's Passing**

43: A Gift From A Stranger

The day before Mother's Day I wanted to purchase flowers for a friend who was hosting a brunch. My mother and I went to the store, but mom waited near the door while I hurried to the floral department to select a bouquet of pink roses for the hostess. We were running late, so I hurriedly walked to our car, but Mamma sort of lingered a few steps behind. Once we settled in the car and I started to drive away, I saw Mamma holding something in her hand. When I asked her what it was, she answered in her sometimes-snappy manner with a little smile on her face, "Some money!" Of course, I was curious because Mamma no longer carries her purse, and definitely **not** money. Too many times, she has left her pocketbook behind, and it is easier to simply take whatever items she may need in my bag.

Naturally, I was curious and asked, "Where did you get the money?" Mamma casually replied, "A lady gave it to me." Now I was very curious and continued to ask, "What lady? Who?" My mother responded, "A

Traveling Down the Road With Grace

lady; I didn't know her." Mamma proceeded to tell me what had previously happened.

"A lady walked up to me, took my hand, and smiled when she placed the money in my hand. Then she said, "Happy Mother's Day, Mother," and she turned around and walked away."

When we arrived at my friend's home, I pulled up to the curb and parked the car. I opened the passenger door for Mamma and gathered the roses from the back seat. While walking together, I asked her, "Do you want me to keep your money? You can buy something for yourself when we go shopping next week." She handed me the bill, and I tucked it in the side of my purse.

Mamma and I arrived at the brunch on time, and it was wonderful. The hostess, a professional singer, serenaded her guests. The music was great. We joined them with some of their songs and we even danced to a few of the popular tunes she sang. Mamma was in the center of the floor, dancing and having the time of her life! Of course, there was an array of sumptuous dishes. Everyone had a wonderful time.

Later that evening, we returned home, and I was emptying my purse when Mamma's *forgotten money* fell out of my bag. Surprisingly, I realized that it was a newly printed twenty-dollar bill! I recalled the incident that occurred in the grocery store earlier that day. Mamma said the lady who gave her the gift was standing near the door, which was next to the floral department. I imagine the lady saw my mother standing there when she entered the store and probably placed the bill in Mamma's palm.

Then she probably said, "Happy Mother's Day, Mother" to her as she turned and left the store. Perhaps, the lady was looking for a "motherly" looking lady, and my mother does have a maternal image, elderly, grey-haired, and slightly stout. I imagined when she saw Mom just standing there, she selected her to receive the gift, and perhaps her task was completed, and she turned and exited from that same door. "What an unusual Mother's Day gift," I thought, "a gift from a stranger on such a special occasion."

Although the gift was given to my mother, I believe it was actually given as a lesson for me, her daughter! Could it be? Perhaps the lady anonymously gave the gift to my mother in memory of her mother? "What a thoughtful and meaningful gesture, a lesson for the daughter, to learn how to repeat "a random act of love, on Mother's Day!" "Could this be the beginning of a new Mother's Day tradition? Well, it is for me. Now that I know how it feels to not have my mother on Mother's Day, I will share a bit of joy with a few other mothers on Mother's Day!

Traveling Down the Road With Grace

Time has passed and Mamma has, too. Mother's Day is approaching. Regardless of my age, the "little girl" in me begins to cry and silently mutters, "I miss my Mamma!" Afterward, God gently reminds me of the joy and peace that Mamma must be having in her Heavenly Home, and that thought is an instant tear-stopper. As I begin to feel better and smile, God reminds me of the lady who gave my mother a $20.00 bill in the grocery store the day before Mother's Day. Thanks to a **Stranger** I have learned to spread a bit of love to a few mothers and grandmothers with $20.00 bills that I give anonymously in memory of my mother on the day before Mother's Day as I wish a **HAPPY MOTHER'S DAY, FROM A STRANGER!**

Traveling Down the Road With Grace

LOVE AND APPRECIATION TO:

Reggie, the best son God could have given me.
Ardina, Sydnee, and Emma,
My Core.
Mackenzie Grace,
Illustrator Extraordinaire.
Ruth Lewis,
Superior Checker.
ALL OF MY DAUGHTERS,
Tremendously Loved Young Ladies.
Oak Cliff Bible Fellowship, Life on Life,
When you heard my story, my book came alive.
Traphene Hickman Library, Director, and Staff,
You called me "author" before I knew I was one.
My family, friends, and prayer partners,
your names are written on my heart and
God knows each of you!
**The Grace of the Lord Jesus be with everyone.
Amen Revelation
22:21
(The last scripture in the Bible)**

THE END

Traveling Down the Road With Grace

ABOUT THE AUTHOR

Traveling Down the Road With Grace

Joann Grandberry was born in Ozark, Alabama, to Grace and Willie Joe Grandberry and later relocated to Gary, Indiana, with her elderly aunt and uncle. She attended Roosevelt School. She later received her B.S. and M.S. degrees in English Education from Indiana University and School Administration from Purdue University. She was employed at the Gary Public Library and United States Steel Corporation and taught at West Side, Roosevelt High Schools, and Calumet College. Joann served as West Side Junior High School's principal and Director of Secondary Education in East Chicago, Indiana.

Her professional writing career began when she won a writing contest offered by the **Gary Post Tribune Newspaper** as a guest editorial writer. She wrote and circulated a weekly newsletter, **Monday Morning Messages,** a publication of inspirational articles that she wrote for homebound patients. The author later wrote two cookbooks, **Miss Grandberry's Great Recipes** and **MOM, Messages of Mothers**, which consist of a variety of stories combined with various recipes from her family members and friends.

Traveling Down the Road With Grace

Later in her life, Joann retired and relocated to Denver, Colorado, and during a visit to her previous hometown, she discovered her mother's declining health and decided to have her return home with her. She became a caregiver for her elderly mother, Grace, who was diagnosed with Alzheimer's and breast cancer. During that time, the mother/daughter team continued traveling and a therapist advised her to journal their experiences, which amazingly grew into the collection of stories that fill the pages of this book.

Join the author and her mother on their numerous journeys. Their stories will inspire, encourage, and entertain you as they board countless trains, buses, airplanes, and automobiles throughout the United States from coast to coast! The book is intertwined with portions of African American culture and traditions woven within their stories as the author delightfully reveals the culture of five generations of her family. Readers will learn a lot, smile occasionally, and just might shed a tear or two.

Joann is an inspirational writer and entertaining storyteller. Enjoy every segment of the book as their journey unfolds throughout their lives. You will be inspired and encouraged as you feel the never-ending love of a mother and daughter.

Join them and experience God's Grace with Grace!

Traveling Down the Road With Grace

Made in the USA
Monee, IL
10 February 2025

11748392R00111